| Genetic Engineering

Other Books in the Current Controversies Series

Abortion
Animal Rights
Bullying
College Admissions
Cybercrime
Deadly Viruses
Death Penalty
Drones, Surveillance, and Targeted Killings
LGBTQ Rights
Medical Ethics
Privacy and Security in the Digital Age
Professional Football
Racial Profiling
Same-Sex Marriage
Violence Against Women

Genetic Engineering

Susan Henneberg, Book Editor

GREENHAVEN
PUBLISHING

Published in 2017 by Greenhaven Publishing, LLC
353 3rd Avenue, Suite 255, New York, NY 10010

Library of Congress Cataloging-in-Publication Data

Names: Henneberg, Susan, editor.
Title: Genetic engineering / edited by Susan Henneberg.
Description: New York : Greenhaven Publishing, 2017. |
Series: Current controversies | Includes index.
Identifiers: LCCN ISBN 9781534500389 (pbk.) | ISBN 9781534500174 (library bound)
Subjects: LCSH: Genetic engineering--Juvenile literature. | Human reproductive
technology--Juvenile literature. | Food--Biotechnology--Juvenile literature.
Classification: LCC QH442.H46 2017 | DDC 576.5--dc23

Manufactured in the United States of America

Website: http://greenhavenpublishing.com

Contents

Chapter 2: Should We Be Afraid of Human Cloning?

Chapter 4: Is the Genetic Engineering of Animals Ethical?

US Food and Drug Administration
Genetically engineered (GE) animals contain additional or altered
genetic material intended to give them new traits or characteristics.
Some produce particular substances such as human insulin for
pharmaceutical use. Other animals can become sources of cells,
tissues, or organs that can be transplanted into humans. GE animals
are regulated by the federal government to assure safety for both
animals and humans.

Yes: Genetic Engineering of Animals Is Ethical

Aaron Saenz
The immense bulk of the Belgian Blue cow is due to selectively
breeding animals with a genetic defect. Traditional selective breeding
is being replaced by genetically engineering animals to produce
breeds with advantageous qualities. This technology could potentially
be used in humans.

Bill Pohlmeier and Alison Van Eenennaam
Scientists can use genetic engineering to fight diseases in animals.
Animal breeders can introduce new genetic sequences into livestock
to increase disease resistance. They can remove specific genes that
cause diseases such as mad cow disease. These approaches can
improve animal well-being and increase the production of safer food.

No: Genetic Engineering of Animals Is Not Ethical

Compassion in World Farming
Genetically modifying animals causes high rates of pre- and post-
natal mortality in cattle and sheep. The animals suffer a large variety
of health problems, such as increased susceptibility to infectious
disease. Many scientists conclude that cloning or genetically
modifying animals is not ethically justified.

  Yourgenome.org

  Among the arguments against GM animals is the risk of new
  diseases spreading from the GM animals to non-GM animals and
  humans. The process of modifying animals puts them at risk for pain,
  deformity, or early death. Some people believe that animals are not a
  product that can be altered for economic benefit.

Foreword

C ontroversy" is a word that has an undeniably unpleasant connotation. It carries a definite negative charge. Controversy can spoil family gatherings, spread a chill around classroom and campus discussion, inflame public discourse, open raw civic wounds, and lead to the ouster of public officials. We often feel that controversy is almost akin to bad manners, a rude and shocking eruption of that which must not be spoken or thought of in polite, tightly guarded society. To avoid controversy, to quell controversy, is often seen as a public good, a victory for etiquette, perhaps even a moral or ethical imperative.

Yet the studious, deliberate avoidance of controversy is also a whitewashing, a denial, a death threat to democracy. It is a false sterilizing and sanitizing and superficial ordering of the messy, ragged, chaotic, at times ugly processes by which a healthy democracy identifies and confronts challenges, engages in passionate debate about appropriate approaches and solutions, and arrives at something like a consensus and a broadly accepted and supported way forward. Controversy is the megaphone, the speaker's corner, the public square through which the citizenry finds and uses its voice. Controversy is the life's blood of our democracy and absolutely essential to the vibrant health of our society.

Our present age is certainly no stranger to controversy. We are consumed by fierce debates about technology, privacy, political correctness, poverty, violence, crime and policing, guns, immigration, civil and human rights, terrorism, militarism, environmental protection, and gender and racial equality. Loudly competing voices are raised every day, shouting opposing opinions, putting forth competing agendas, and summoning starkly different visions of a utopian or dystopian future. Often these voices attempt to shout the others down; there is precious little listening and considering among the cacophonous din. Yet listening and considering, too, are essential to the health of a democracy. If controversy is democracy's lusty lifeblood, respectful listening and careful thought are its higher faculties, its brain, its conscience.

Current Controversies does not shy away from or attempt to hush the loudly competing voices. It seeks to provide readers with as wide and representative as possible a range of articulate voices on any given controversy of the day, separates each one out to allow it to be heard clearly and fairly, and encourages careful listening to each of these well-crafted, thoughtfully expressed opinions, supplied by some of today's leading academics, thinkers, analysts, politicians, policy makers, economists, activists, change agents, and advocates. Only after listening to a wide range of opinions on an issue, evaluating the strengths and weaknesses of each argument, assessing how well the facts and available evidence mesh with the stated opinions and conclusions, and thoughtfully and critically examining one's own beliefs and conscience can the reader begin to arrive at his or her own conclusions and articulate his or her own stance on the spotlighted controversy.

This process is facilitated and supported in each Current Controversies volume by an introduction and chapter overviews that provide readers with the essential context they need to begin engaging with the spotlighted controversies, with the debates surrounding them, and with their own perhaps shifting or nascent opinions on them. Chapters are organized around several key questions that are answered with diverse opinions representing all points on the political spectrum. In its content, organization, and methodology, readers are encouraged to determine the authors' point of view and purpose, interrogate and analyze the various arguments and their rhetoric and structure, evaluate the arguments' strengths and weaknesses, test their claims against available facts and evidence, judge the validity of the reasoning, and bring into clearer, sharper focus the reader's own beliefs and conclusions and how they may differ from or align with those in the collection or those of classmates.

Research has shown that reading comprehension skills improve dramatically when students are provided with compelling, intriguing, and relevant "discussable" texts. The subject matter of these collections could not be more compelling, intriguing, or urgently relevant to today's students and the world they are poised to inherit. The anthologized articles also provide the basis for stimulating, lively, and passionate classroom debates. Students who are compelled to anticipate objections to their own argument and identify the flaws in those of an opponent read more carefully, think more critically, and steep themselves in relevant context, facts, and information more thoroughly. In short, using discussable text of the kind provided by every single volume in the Current Controversies series encourages close reading, facilitates reading comprehension, fosters research, strengthens critical thinking, and greatly enlivens and energizes classroom discussion and participation. The entire learning process is deepened, extended, and strengthened.

If we are to foster a knowledgeable, responsible, active, and engaged citizenry, we must provide readers with the intellectual, interpretive, and critical-thinking tools and experience necessary to make sense of the world around them and of the all-important debates and arguments that inform it. We must encourage them not to run away from or attempt to quell controversy but to embrace it in a responsible, conscientious, and thoughtful way, to sharpen and strengthen their own informed opinions by listening to and critically analyzing those of others. This series encourages respectful engagement with and analysis of current controversies and competing opinions and fosters a resulting increase in the strength and rigor of one's own opinions and stances. As such, it helps readers assume their rightful place in the public square and provides them with the skills necessary to uphold their awesome responsibility—guaranteeing the continued and future health of a vital, vibrant, and free democracy.

Introduction

"Genetic engineering applications are emerging rapidly, producing fierce debates in the US and the rest of the world."

On July 1, 2016, Vermont became the first state in the US to require the labeling of genetically modified ingredients in most food products on grocery store shelves. This rule had nationwide impact. The US had no regulations regarding GMO food. However, major food companies did not want to manufacture different foods or different labels for one small state. Companies with products such as Campbell soups, Kellogg's cereals, and Mars candy bars put one of these phrases on all their labels: "partially produced with genetic engineering," "may be produced with genetic engineering," or "produced with genetic engineering." Food sold in bulk have labels on shelves or bins. The Vermont law generated a nationwide debate about the safety of eating genetically modified plants and animals. Scientists, however, are concerned about a bigger issue. How can genetic engineering be applied to humans?

Genetically modifying plants and animals is nothing new. For thousands of years, farmers have been modifying plants and animals through selective breeding. Seedless watermelons, purple roses, and purebred dogs are examples of how humans have enhanced desirable traits in organisms. Modern technology has now allowed scientists to modify genes at the molecular level, using gene splicing, gene manipulation, or recombinant DNA technology. Scientists can use enzymes to remove or add DNA to alter genes. Genes from one organism can be removed and inserted into another organism, using a type of "gene gun." For instance, a gene from a bacterium can be inserted into a tomato plant to make it resistant to insects.

Genetic engineering has been widely used in American agriculture. Farmers claim that genetically modified organisms (GMOs) have produced higher crop yields, reduced farm costs, increased farm profits, and brought improvements in health and the environment. In 2016, according to the US Department of Agriculture, 89 percent of corn, 94 percent of soybeans, and 89 percent of cotton was modified to be herbicide tolerant. Farmers can kill weeds without killing the crop. These crops have found their way into American grocery stores in processed foods such as snack foods, sweetened drinks, and breakfast cereals.

GMO proponents say that new crops will benefit consumers around the world. Farmers will be able to grow papayas that repel viruses, corn that survives drought, soybeans that withstand herbicides, and potatoes that don't bruise. GMO supporters claim that as the world population grows, GMO foods will make enough nutritious food to feed everyone despite limited land, water, and other resources.

Not everyone believes that GMO foods are safe or desirable. GMO opponents claim that genetically modified crops can harm the environment. The anti-GMO Institute for Responsible Technology says that GM crops "reduce bio-diversity, pollute water resources, and are unsustainable." Some farmers worry that GMO crops might cross-breed with the naturally existing populations from which they are derived. Consumers who want non-GMO food might not be able to find it. Some scientists are concerned that GMO food could cause dangerous allergic reactions in susceptible people.

Genetically modified animals are another controversial product of the science of genetic engineering. As in plants, genes can be inserted, deleted, or recombined into animal genomes to create animals with select characteristics. GM mice have been used for decades in medical labs to study obesity, heart disease, diabetes, arthritis, substance abuse, aging, and Parkinson disease. GM pigs soon might be suitable organ donors for humans. Goats have been modified to produce malaria vaccine in their milk. Glow-in-the-dark fish can warn people of pollutants in water.

Fast growing salmon, featherless chickens, less flatulent cows, and super muscular pigs have also been developed.

The next step after genetically modifying, some scientists believe, is the cloning of animals. To clone an animal, scientists remove a cell from the animal they want to copy. They then insert the DNA of the donor animal's cell into another animal's egg cell that has had its own DNA-containing nucleus removed. The egg develops into an embryo in the science lab, and then is implanted into a surrogate mother animal. If the mother gives birth, the newborn has the same genetic makeup of the donor animal. This is the process that was used to produce the first cloned animal, Dolly the sheep, in England in 1996.

When news of Dolly's birth was released, scientists, researchers, and many other people became excited about the possibilities in animal cloning. One Korean biotechnology company offered to clone pets for a high fee, though it warned consumers that the animals produced may have different characteristics than the original because of the influence of environment. Livestock producers looked into methods of reproducing particularly high-performing animals. Some scientists researched ways to clone animals that are near extinction before they are lost forever. Cloning animals is notoriously difficult, however, with an average success rate of less than 5 percent.

After Dolly's birth, there was much discussion of the logical next step in cloning, that of cloning humans. Therapeutic cloning, in which human cells are cloned, has shown promise in creating embryonic stem cells. These cells could be used in stem cell therapy to treat diseases, spinal cord injury, blindness, infertility, and more. Another use for therapeutic cloning is to create organs and tissues to improve or replace damaged human tissue. Reproductive cloning is much more controversial. It involves making an entire cloned human, instead of specific cells or tissues. Though many countries and some US states have banned reproductive cloning, in 2015 there were no federal laws banning it in the US.

Genetic engineering applications are emerging rapidly, producing fierce debates in the US and the rest of the world. The controversies are explored in this volume with chapters titled "Should the Genetic Engineering of Babies Be Prohibited?" "Should We Be Afraid of Human Cloning?" "Is Genetically Modified Food Good for the World?" and "Is the Genetic Engineering of Animals Ethical?" Articles from a variety of viewpoints will allow readers to decide for themselves the answers to these important questions.

CHAPTER 1

Should the Genetic Engineering of Babies Be Prohibited?

Overview: Genetic Engineering of "Designer Babies" May Soon Be Possible

Sally Deneen

Sally Deneen is a Seattle-based freelance journalist and editor.

The Human Genetic Blueprint Has Been Drafted, Offering Both Perils and Opportunities for the Environment. The Big Question: Are We Changing the Nature of Nature?

Princeton University microbiologist Lee M. Silver can see a day a few centuries from now when there are two species of humans—the standard-issue "Naturals," and the "Gene-enriched," an elite class whose parents consciously bought for them designer genes, and whose parents before them did the same, and so on for generations. Want Billy to have superior athletic ability? Plunk down the cash. Want Suzy to be exceptionally smart? Just pull out the Visa card at your local fertility clinic, where the elite likely will go to enhance their babies-to-be. It will start innocently enough: Birth defects that are caused by a single gene, such as cystic fibrosis and Tay-Sachs disease, will be targeted first, and probably with little controversy. Then, as societal fears about messing with Mother Nature subside, Silver and other researchers predict that a genetic solution to preventing diabetes, heart disease and other big killers will be found and offered. So will genetic inoculations against HIV. Eventually, the mind will be targeted for improvement—preventing alcohol addiction and mental illness, and enhancing visual acuity or intelligence to try to produce the next Vincent Van Gogh or Albert Einstein. Even traits from other animals may be added, such as a dog's sense of smell or an eagle's eyesight.

What parents would see as a simple, if pricey, way to improve their kids would result, after many generations of gene selection, in a profound change by the year 2400—humans would be two

"Designer People," by Sally Deneen, The Environmental Magazine. Reprinted by permission.

distinct species, related as humans and chimps are today, and just as unable to interbreed. People now have 46 chromosomes; the gene-enriched would have 48 to accommodate added traits, Silver predicts in his aptly titled book, Remaking Eden.

We may already be on the path to change the very nature of nature. If you think it's a far-off prospect best left to future generations, think again. On June 26, 2000, with much fanfare, scientists with the taxpayer-supported Human Genome Project (working with the private Celera Genomics of Rockville, Maryland) announced that they had completed a working draft of a genetic blueprint for a human being. Many details still need to be filled in before scientists can build a human from scratch.

Sequencing the human genome requires identifying 3.2 billion chemical "letters" located on the 46 coiled strands of DNA found in nearly every human cell. While researchers now know the order in which DNA is arranged on the chromosomes, they haven't identified all those chemical "letters," which contain the instructions for making the proteins that comprise the human body. About half of the genome sequence is in near-finished form or better; a quarter is finished. The 15-year project is to be completed in 2005 at a budgeted cost of $3 billion, though some of that tax money is spent on other genomic research.

While the implications for longevity, health insurance and discrimination of this milestone achievement have grabbed media attention, the ramifications for the environment—good and bad— haven't.

An Accelerating Timetable

How soon will all this happen? Silver believes that by around 2010 parents will be able to genetically ensure their babies won't grow up to be fat or alcoholic, and by 2050 arrange to insert an extra gene into single-cell embryos within 24 hours of conception to make babies resistant to AIDS. It is already possible to insert foreign DNA into mice, pigs and sheep. The obstacles to inserting them in humans are mainly technical ones. At this point in human knowledge, it could lead to mutations. Several techniques are under development to try to avoid that, however.

"For the near and midterm future, we're looking at science fiction. You'd have to be terminally reckless to do that type of human engineering on people [with what we know now]," argues law professor Henry T. Greely, co-director of the Program in Genomics, Ethics and Society at the Stanford University Center for Biomedical Ethics.

To change a baby's eye color or hair color within a fertilized human egg "would be a very expensive and dangerous proposition for such trivial purposes," says Dr. Marvin Frazier, who fields human genome questions as director of the Life Sciences Division of the U.S. Department of Energy's Office of Biological and Environmental Research. "It is also my opinion that this would be wrong," he added, "but that will not stop some people from wanting to try."

As for manipulating intelligence or athletic ability, Frazier says it will take scientists many decades to figure out how to do it. These particular traits don't rely on one gene, but on all genes. They also rely "to a significant degree" on nurture instead of nature. Even when scientists figure it out, "It is likely that to achieve the desired goals would require a lot of experimentation, which translates into many hundred or thousands of mistakes before you get it right." That means, Frazier says, "a lot of malformed babies and miscarriages."

A Pivotal Moment

To University of Washington professor Phil Bereano, among others, now is the time for all of us to talk with friends and colleagues to hash out the ethical and societal implications of this Brave New World. Do we really want to commodify people? Could it be a Pandora's box? Unfortunately, the box may already be open: Many nations have banned genetic engineering on humans, but the United States has not.

"If scientists don't play God, who will?" said supporter James Watson, former head of the Human Genome Project, speaking before the British Parliamentary and Scientific Committee in June.

"The key question is not whether human [genetic] manipulation will occur, but how and when it will," says a confident Gregory Stock, director of UCLA's Program on Science, Technology and Society in a report entitled, "The Prospects for Human Germline Engineering."

Meanwhile, a long-anticipated September report by the American Association for the Advancement of Science (AAAS) surprised some observers by failing to call for a ban on making inheritable genetic changes in humans—that is, genetic changes that would be carried on by progeny. Indeed, while the report says that such research "cannot presently be carried out safely and responsibly on human beings," it also leaves wiggle room. "Human trials of inheritable genetic changes should not be initiated until reliable techniques for gene correction or replacement are developed that meet agreed-upon standards for safety and efficacy," says report co-author Mark Frankel, director of AAAS' Scientific Freedom, Responsibility and Law Program.

Noting the public outcry after the cloning of Dolly the sheep—which raised the possibility of cloned human beings—the report stresses the importance of public discussion about genetic research before major technical innovations occur. So instead of a ban, the report suggests "rigorous analysis and public dialogue."

But there's no shortage of opposition to human engineering. The San Francisco-based Exploratory Initiative on the New Human Genetic Technologies seeks, among other things, to alert a largely unwitting public to what is going on. "It really is a nightmare vision," says Rich Hayes, who coordinates the campaign from his Public Media Center office. "Once we start genetically re-engineering human beings, where would we stop? We should have the maturity and wisdom to ban the modification of the genes we pass to our children."

Designer Genes

The futuristic notion of choosing a child's genes from a catalog can certainly capture the imagination. Just as parents today enroll their children in the best possible schools and pay for orthodontics, the parents of the future—perhaps in a few decades—would be able to choose from an ever-increasing suite of traits: hair color, eye color, bigger muscles and so on.

Maybe they'd like to add a few inches to a child's height. Or improve a kid's chances at longevity by tweaking inherited DNA. Or ensure a resistance to viruses. Neighborhood clinics could, by appointment, insert a block of genes into a newly fertilized egg. As one cell broke into two, then four, and so on, each cell would contain the new traits. And the child would pass on those traits to all subsequent generations. Who could blame parents for going for this?

But to Stuart Newman, professor of cell biology and anatomy at New York Medical College in Valhalla, New York, the effect on human biology could be analogous to transforming wild areas into artificial areas, or wild food into artificial food.

We "might be changing people into products—genetically engineered products," says Newman, who also is chairman of the Human Genetics Committee for the Council for Responsible Genetics in Cambridge, Massachusetts. "That's something that's opened up by the Humane Genome Project."

"We believe that certain activities in the area of genetics and cloning should be prohibited because they violate basic environmental and ethical principles," Friends of the Earth President Brent Blackwelder and Physicians for Social Responsibility Executive Director Robert Musil said in a 1999 joint statement. "The idea of redesigning human beings and animals to suit the primarily commercial goals of a limited number of individuals is fundamentally at odds with the principle of respect for nature."

Proponents and critics alike envision a future in which those who can't afford gene enrichment will be relegated to second-class citizenship. "As far as I'm concerned, this thrill we have about the future will end up being one big elitist ripple," says Beth Burrows, director of the Edmonds Institute, a suburban Seattle nonprofit institute that works on issues related to environment, technology, ethics and law.

The Green Dimension

And what about the environment? Burrows says several important questions arise about genetic tampering: What are we creating? How will it affect the natural world? What will be the effect on evolution for each species involved? How will it change feeding patterns, or food for other animals? Without understanding interactions, she says, "We may do some extremely stupid things. If people are concerned that there was such a severe backlash against genetically modified foods, I think they haven't seen anything compared to the backlash when we are able to alter the human genome in significant ways—even insignificant ways," says Burrows.

UCLA's Gregory Stock agrees the impact of human genetic modification is profound, but he likes it. "This technology will force us to re-examine even the very notion of what it means to be human," he wrote in a recent report. "For as we become subject to the same process of conscious design that has so dramatically altered the world around us, we will be unable to avoid looking at what distinguishes us from other life, at how our genetics shapes us, at how much we are willing to intervene in life's flow from parent to child."

Ignacio Chapela of University of California at Berkeley is troubled by still other implications the Human Genome Project may bring for the natural world—including plants engineered specifically to produce human proteins, and pigs produced to have antigens that are more human-like in a quest to help humans. To Chapela, a professor in the Department of Environmental Science, Policy and Management, the concept, say, of using chimpanzees as surrogate mothers for human embryos is "abhorrent—degrading for chimpanzees, and for humans, as well. I think what we're talking about is a very deep understanding of what it means to be part of an intricate web of life, and why we have boundaries between species." To Chapela, proponents see the world as a sphere smeared with mix-and-match DNA. "Evolutionarily, it makes sense to have boundaries," he says, "and we're just willy-nilly breaking them down."

A Brave New World

None of these developments will occur in a vacuum; great advancements in robotics are also expected, portending a trend toward the melding of man and machine in a quest for greater human longevity—to age 110, 130 and beyond. UCLA's Stock dubs this new human/machine "Metaman," a "global superorganism." If it seems like mere musings stolen from a science-fiction film, consider this bit of reality: In March, Berkeley researchers announced that they had invented the first "bionic chip"—part living tissue, part machine. Eventually, such chips and circuitry could help in the development of body implants for treating genetic diseases such as diabetes.

"It's a key discovery because it's the first step to building complex circuitry that incorporates the living cell," mechanical engineering professor Boris Rubinsky, who created the device with a graduate student, said afterward. "The first electronic diode made it possible to have the computer. Who knows what the first biological diode will make possible?"

UCLA's Stock isn't concerned about the effects of human genetic engineering on nature. "Even if half the world's species were lost, enormous diversity would still remain," he argues in his 1993 book, Metaman: The Merging of Humans and Machines into a Global Superorganism. "We best serve ourselves, as well as future generations, by focusing on the short-term consequences of our actions rather than our vague notions about the needs of the distant future." If medical science develops an easy cure for cancer, [nuclear] wastes may not be viewed as a significant health hazard after all. If robots can be employed to safely concentrate and reprocess the radioactive materials, they might even be valuable."

Not so fast, says another architect of the modern world, Bill Joy, the father of Java software and co-founder of Sun Microsystems. Joy posits with some feeling of guilt that "our most powerful 21st-century technologies" are threatening to make humans an endangered species." In a celebrated article in Wired magazine last year, Joy blamed the possible extinction of humans on a few key causes, including genetic engineering and robotics. Artificial intelligence should match that of humans within 20 or 30 years.

To combat the perceived inevitability of this Brave New World, Marcy Darnovsky, a Sonoma State University instructor who works with the Exploratory Initiative on the New Human Genetic Technologies, calls for three things: First, a global ban on inheritable genetic engineering on humans; second, a global ban on human reproductive cloning; and third, an effective and accountable regulation of other human genetic technologies.

Burrows says we need to be pondering such weighty questions as: Do we really want to merge with machines? "There are tremendous—awful—choices to be made," she says. "It's very risky to have these discussions because they're about common values. The subject is difficult, painful and easily avoided. But we have to stop focusing on the science and think of ourselves as part of an ecosystem."

Chapela is also worried about the lack of civic discourse. But the advocates are talking, particularly among themselves. At a Berkeley conference, one of them, Extropy Institute President Max More, stood before the crowd and read an open letter to Mother Nature:

Sorry to disturb you, but we humans—your offspring—come to you with some things to say:

You have raised us from simple self-replicating chemicals to trillion-celled mammals;

What you have made us is glorious, yet deeply flawed.

We will no longer tolerate the tyranny of aging and death. Through genetic alterations, cellular manipulations, synthetic organs, and any necessary means, we will endow ourselves with enduring vitality and remove our expiration date."

Other proponents are more sober, and include Nobel laureate scientists. "This is no 'marginal' movement or way of thinking," Chapela says. "The group advocating human re-engineering includes extremely powerful, influential and wealthy people. So don't expect them to roll over easily or soon."

Genetically Modifying Humans Can Have Unforeseen Consequences

Satyajit Patra and Araromi Adewale Andrew

Satyajit Patra and Araromi Adewale Andrew are on the faculty of the American International Medical University in St. Lucia.

INTRODUCTION

Human genetic engineering relies heavily on science and technology. It was developed to help end the spread of diseases. With the advent of genetic engineering, scientists can now change the way genomes are constructed to terminate certain diseases that occur as a result of genetic mutation [1]. Today genetic engineering is used in fighting problems such as cystic fibrosis, diabetes, and several other diseases. Another deadly disease now being treated with genetic engineering is the "bubble boy" disease (Severe Combined Immunodeficiency). This is a clear indication that genetic engineering has the potential to improve the quality of life and allow for longer life span [2].

Clearly, one of the greatest benefits of this field is the prospect of helping cure illness and diseases in unborn children. Having a genetic screening with a fetus can allow for treatment of the unborn. Overtime this can impact the growing spread of diseases in future generations.

However, these benefits are not without peril. Human genetic engineering is a development that people are either very passionate about or opposed to completely. This article gives a brief account on the effect of this principle on the biosphere together with several controversial issues that accompany the acceptance of this technology [3]. The manuscript has been prepared by using information from peer reviewed journals indexed in pubmed in the period of 2000 to 2015.

Effects on the Environment

Although the positive impacts of this field could be enormous, there are many questions raised that needs to be answered. New organisms created by genetic engineering could present an ecological problem. One cannot predict the changes that a genetically engineered species would make on the environment. The release of a new genetically engineered species would also have the possibility of causing an imbalance in the ecology of a region just exotic species would do. An accident or an unknown result could cause several problems. An accident in engineering the genetics of a virus or bacteria for example could result in a stronger type, which could cause a serious epidemic when released. This could be fatal in human genetic engineering creating problems ranging from minor medical problems, to death [4].

Effects on Human

Looking at the fact that genetic engineering employs viral vector that carries functional gene inside the human body; the repercussion are still unknown. There are no clues as to where functional genes are being placed. They may even replace the important genes, instead of mutated genes. Thus, this may lead to another health condition or disease to human. Also, as defective genes are replaced with functional gene, then it is expected that there will be a reduction in genetic diversity and if human beings will have identical genomes, the population as a whole will be susceptible to virus or any form of diseases [5].

Genetic engineering could also create unknown side effects or outcomes. Certain changes in a plant or animal could cause unpredicted allergic reactions in some people which, in its original form, did not occur. Other changes could result into the toxicity of an organism to humans or other organisms.

Antibiotic Resistance

Genetic engineering often uses genes for antibiotic resistance as "selectable markers." Early in the engineering process, these markers help identify cells that have taken up foreign genes. Although they have no further use, the genes continue to be expressed in plant tissues. Most genetically engineered plant foods carry fully functioning antibiotic-resistance genes.

The presence of antibiotic-resistance genes in foods could have lethal effects. Therefore, eating these foods could reduce the effectiveness of antibiotics to fight disease when these antibiotics are taken with meals. More so, the resistance genes could be transferred to human or animal pathogens, making them impervious to antibiotics. If transfer were to occur, it could aggravate the already serious health problem of antibioticresistant disease organisms [6].

Ethical and Social Issues

"Playing God" has become a strong argument against genetic engineering. Several issues have also been raised as regards the acceptance of this technology. These concerns range from ethical issues to lack of knowledge on the effects genetic engineering may have. One major concern is that once an altered gene is placed in an organism, the process cannot be reversed. Public reaction to the use of rDNA in genetic engineering has been mixed. The production of medicines through the use of genetically altered organisms has generally been welcomed. However, critics of rDNA fear that disease-producing organisms used in some rDNA experiments might develop extremely infectious forms that could cause worldwide epidemics [7].

As more human genes are being used in non-human organisms to create new forms of life that are genetically partly human, new ethical questions arise. For instance, what percentage of human genes does an organism have to contain before it is considered human and how many human genes would a green pepper for example have to contain before it can be eaten without qualms. Human genes are now being inserted into tomatoes and peppers to make them grow faster [8]. This suggests that one can now be a vegetarian and a cannibal at the same time. For meateaters, the same question could be posed about eating pork with human genes. What about the mice that have been genetically engineered to produce human sperm [9]. The question is what psychological effect would it pose on the offspring?

Critics have questioned the safety of genetically engineered bovine somatotropin (BST) to increase the milk yield of dairy cows (BST) for both the cows that are injected with it and the humans who drink the resulting milk; owing to the fact that it increases a cow's likelihood of developing mastitis, or infection of the udder, and it also makes cows more susceptible to infertility and lameness [6].

Transgenic plants also present controversial issues. Allergens can be transferred from one food crop to another through genetic engineering. Another concern is that pregnant women eating genetically modified products may endanger their offspring by harming normal fetal development and altering gene expression [10].

In 2002 the National Academy of Sciences released a report calling for a legal ban on human cloning [11]. The report concluded that the high rate of health problems in cloned animals suggests that such an effort in humans would be highly dangerous for the mother and developing embryo and is likely to fail. Beyond safety, the possibility of cloning humans also raises a variety of social issues like the psychological issues that would result for a cloned child who is the identical twin of his or her parent.

Another frightening scenario is the destructive use of genetic engineering. Terrorist groups or armies could develop more powerful biological weaponry. These weapons could be resistant to medicines, or even targeted at people who carry certain genes. Genetically engineered organisms used for biological weapons might also reproduce faster, which would create larger quantities in shorter periods of time, increasing the level of devastation [12].

Conclusion

Despite all of these current concerns, the potential for genetic engineering is tremendous. However, further testing and research will be required to educate society on the pros and cons of genetic engineering. There is no doubt that this technology will continue to present intriguing and difficult challenges for 21st century scientists and ethicists, and education and meaningful, respectful discourse are just the starting point of what is required to tackle such complex ethical issues. With the newfound breakthroughs in cloning, the capabilities of changing human characteristics are unpredictable. We can then anticipate intense cross-disciplinary debate and discussion as new life forms are emanating through science and medicine [13].

References

1. Patra SAA (2015) Effects of Genetic Engineering - The Ethical and Social Implications. Annals of Clinical and Laboratory Research.
2. Fischer A, Hacein-Bey S, Cavazzana-Calvo M (2002) Gene therapy of severe combined immunodeficiencies. Nat Rev Immunol 2: 615-621.
3. D'Halluin K, Ruiter R (2013) Directed genome engineering for genome optimization. Int J DevBiol 57:621-627.
4. Mercer DK, Scott KP, Bruce-Johnson WA, Glover LA, Flint HJ (1999) Fate of free DNA and transformation of the oral bacterium Streptococcus gordonii DL1 by plasmid DNA in human saliva. Appl Environ Microbiol65:6-10.
5. Jr FW (1996) Viral Genetics. In: Medical Microbiology. 4th Edition edn. University of Texas Medical Branch at Galveston.
6. Mepham TB (2000) The role of food ethics in food policy. The Proceedings of the Nutrition Society 59:609-618.
7. Deuschle K, Fehr M, Hilpert M, Lager I, Lalonde S, et al. (2005) Genetically encoded sensors for metabolites. Cytometry A 64:3-9.
8. Youm JW, Jeon JH, Kim H, Kim YH, Ko K, et al. (2008) Transgenic tomatoes expressing human beta-amyloid for use as a vaccine against Alzheimer›s disease. Biotechnollett30: 1839-1845.
9. Naz RK (2009) Development of genetically engineered human sperm immunocontraceptives. J reprodimmunol, 83:145-150.
10. Smith JM (2003) Seeds of Deception: Exposing Industry and Government Lies About the Safety of the Genetically Engineered Foods You›re Eating.
11. Powledge TM (2002) Will they throw the bath water out with the baby?: The US Congress is still debating whether to outlaw cloning humans. EMBO Reports 3:209-211.
12. Sayler GS, Ripp S (2000) Field applications of genetically engineered microorganisms for bioremediation processes. Curropin in biotechnol 11:286-289.
13. Powledge TM (2002) Will they throw the bath water out with the baby? The US Congress is still debating whether to outlaw cloning humans. EMBO Rep 3:209-211.

Human Traits Are Too Complex to Be Genetically Modified

A Cecile JW Janssens

A Cecile JW Janssens is a research professor of epidemiology at Emory University in Atlanta, Georgia.

This week, scientists gathered in Washington, DC for the International Summit on Human Gene Editing to discuss a technology called CRISPR-CAS9, which can insert, remove and change the DNA of basically any organism. It is relatively simple, inexpensive and accurate, and it's already being used in laboratories around the world to make cells and breed laboratory animals with modified DNA for the study of diseases.

CRISPR could also be used to modify DNA in human embryos, but the question is whether this should be allowed. Among the concerns scientists and bioethicists have highlighted are heritable gene modifications and the use of this technology to create "designer babies." CRISPR provides new opportunities for disease treatment and prevention, but with unknown and potentially substantial risks that warrant an ethical discussion. And this discussion should be rooted in an understanding of what can and cannot be meaningfully edited.

I study the genetic prediction of complex diseases and traits. Research in my field has consistently shown that human traits and common diseases are not genetic enough to be predicted using DNA tests. For the same reasons, it will be impossible to successfully program the presence of traits in embryos.

Any concerns that CRISPR could taken a step further to enhance babies by selecting favorable traits such as intelligence and athleticism may be unwarranted.

What can be edited?

The first (and failed) experiment of human embryo editing aimed to repair a single gene mutation for beta-thalassemia, a severe blood disorder. Other diseases mentioned as future targets for gene editing, such as sickle cell disease and Duchenne muscular dystrophy, are caused by single gene mutations.

These diseases are—at least hypothetically—easier to fix because the cause is entirely genetic and simple. For these diseases, research using CRISPR may lead to breakthrough discoveries for therapies and, potentially, for prevention.

But genetic editing of embryos for single-gene disorders also warrants caution. Not only could off-target cuts—unintended edits in the wrong places of the DNA—introduce heritable errors, but mutations may have so-called antagonistic pleiotropic effects.

This means that the expression of the gene increases the risk of one disease while decreasing the risk of another. Take beta-thalassemia or sickle cell disease, for example: carrying two mutated copies leads to severe illness, but carrying one mutated copy reduces the risk of fatal malaria.

There is still much we don't know about our genome.

Why traits cannot be designed in embryos

For a trait to be "programmed" with gene editing, it needs to meet two criteria.

First, the traits must be predominantly determined by DNA, which means that their heritability needs to be close to 100%. The lower the heritability, the more nongenetic factors such as lifestyle, education and stress play a role. The less likely the trait can be genetically programmed.

Parents who wish to *enhance* their offspring may be particularly risk-averse when it comes to the unknown adverse consequences of genome editing. That means that the heritability of favorable traits may need to be very close to 100%.

But a recent review, summarizing 50 years of heritability research, showed that only a few traits and diseases had an estimated heritability higher than 90%. Intelligence and higher-level cognitive function were around 50%, muscle power at 70% and temperament and personality at around 45%.

Second, the "genetic architecture" must be straightforward. Traits must be caused by a single mutation, like beta-thalassemia, or by an interaction between a limited number of mutations. It may technically become possible to edit DNA accurately at multiple places in the near future. But we still won't know what exactly needs to be edited to program a trait when tens or hundreds of gene variants are involved.

Gene editing for favorable traits is not just a matter of tweaking the genes in the right direction. What makes people intelligent, for instance, isn't a combination of the "right genes" and the "right environment," but the "right combination" of genes and environment. Since the future environment of the embryo is unknown at the moment of editing, it will be impossible to know what the right genes need to be.

This is why the traits people might want to enhance can't be programmed in the embryo, not even with the most accurate and reliable version of CRISPR. The technology is not the limitation for enhancing babies—nature is.

Despite the successes in gene discovery of the past 10 years, our knowledge of the combined contribution of all genetic variants is too limited for embryo editing. Even when all genes and their complex interactions are completely understood, our ability to use gene editing for favorable traits will remain limited because human traits are just not genetic enough.

We need to be clear about what cannot be edited

Urged by concerns about the safety and reliability of CRISPR technology and the unknown medical, societal, environmental and ethical consequences of human gene editing, a group of scientists are calling for a voluntary moratorium on "attempts at germline genome modification of clinical application in humans."

The UNESCO International Bioethics Committee has also called for a moratorium citing concern over the creation of "heritable modifications" and "enhancing individuals." Interestingly, their report acknowledges that CRISPR:

> could be a watershed in the history of medicine [...] even though it must be noted that there are only a few diseases for which the abnormality of one single gene is a necessary and sufficient condition.

This little side note, however, marks the boundaries of what can meaningfully be edited in the DNA of an embryo.

Gene editing technology warrants further study and refinement, which should be accompanied by evaluations of potential adverse consequences. But progress should not be hindered by an ethical debate about a potential misuse of the technology that will not be possible.

Polygenic diseases and traits are simultaneously too complex genetically and not genetic enough. This limits the opportunities for disease prediction, and will also prevent the genetic enhancement of babies.

Genetically Editing Human Embryos Can Have Positive Effects

Julian Savulescu

Julian Savulescu holds the Uehiro Chair in Practical Ethics and is director of the Uehiro Centre for Practical Ethics at Oxford, director of the Oxford Centre for Neuroethics, and director of the Program on the Ethics of the New Biosciences.

Scientists from around the world are meeting in Washington this week to debate how best to proceed with research into gene-editing technology.

Gene editing is a new precise form of genetic engineering. It uses enzymes from bacteria to locate genes within DNA and delete or replace them. In early 2015, Chinese scientists used it to modify human embryos as a first step towards preventing the genetic transmission of a blood disease.

Many people, including scientists, are worried about creating genetically modified humans. They're worried about numerous things: genetic mistakes being passed on to the next generation; the creation of designer babies who are more intelligent, more beautiful or more athletic; and the possibility of causing severe growth abnormalities or cancer.

While these are valid concerns, they don't justify a ban on research. Indeed, such research is a moral imperative for five reasons.

"Five Reasons We Should Embrace Gene-editing Research on Human Embryos," Julian Savulescu, The Conversation, December 3, 2015. http://phys.org/news/2015-12-embrace -gene-editing-human-embryos.html. Licensed under CC BY ND 4.0 International.

1. Curing genetic diseases

Gene editing could be used to cure genetic diseases such cystic fibrosis or thalassaemia (the blood disease that the Chinese researchers were working to eliminate). At present, there are no cures for such diseases.

Detractors say selection of healthy embryos or fetuses via genetic testing is preferable. But such genetic tests require abortion or embryo destruction, which is also objectionable to some people.

What's more, genetic selection doesn't benefit patients—it's not a cure. It merely brings a different person, who is free from disease, into existence. Future people would be grateful if their disease is cured, rather than being replaced by a different healthier or non-disabled person.

2. Dealing with complex diseases

Most common human diseases, such as heart disease or schizophrenia, don't just involve one gene that's abnormal (such as in cystic fibrosis). They're the result of many, sometimes hundreds, of genes combining to cause ill health.

Genetic selection technologies can't eliminate genetic predispositions to these diseases. In principle, gene editing could be used to reduce the risk of heart disease or Alzheimer's disease.

3. Delaying or stopping ageing

Each day, thousands of people die from age-related causes. Cardiovascular disease (strongly age-related) is emerging as the biggest cause of death in the developing world. Ageing kills 30 million every year.

That makes it the most under-researched cause of death and suffering relative to its significance. Indeed, age-related diseases, such as heart disease or cancer, are really the symptoms of an underlying disease: ageing.

Gene editing could delay or arrest ageing; this has already been achieved in mice. Gene editing might offer the prospect of humans living twice as long, or perhaps even hundreds of years, without loss of memory, frailty or impotence.

4. Stopping the genetic lottery

The fourth reason for supporting gene-editing research on human embryos is the flip side of the designer baby objection. People worry that such technology could be used to create a master race, like fair-haired, blue-eyed "Aryans."

What this concern neglects is that the biological lottery—i.e. nature—has no mind to fairness. Some are born gifted and talented, others with short painful lives or severe disabilities. While we may worry about the creation of a genetic masterclass, we should also be concerned about those who draw the short genetic straw.

Diet, education, special services and other social interventions are used to correct natural inequality. Ritalin, for example, is prescribed to up to 10% of children with poor self-control to improve their educational prospects and behavioural control.

Gene editing could be used as a part of public health care for egalitarian reasons: to benefit the worst off. People worry that such technologies will be used to benefit only those who can afford it—keep reading for why they shouldn't.

5. Making disease treatments less costly

Gene editing of human embryos could enable greater understanding of disease and new treatments that don't modify human beings.

Gene-edited embryonic stem cell lines that cause or protect against disease could help us understand the origins of disease. Other edited stem cells could help treatment—imagine blood cells that kill and replace leukemic cells.

This knowledge could be used to develop treatments for diseases, including drugs, that can be produced cheaply. And that would reduce, rather than increase, inequality.

The moral imperative

There are valid concerns about applying gene editing to create live born babies. Such reproductive applications could be banned.

But the technology could be used for therapeutic research: to understand disease and develop new treatments. And any constraints we place on it must keep this in mind.

Laws to prevent reproductive gene editing may be justified on the basis of safety concerns but a ban on therapeutic gene editing cannot.

To ban it would be to ignore a great deal of good that can be done for a great many people, including some of the most vulnerable.

"Designer Babies" Can Have a Positive Impact on Society

Paul Waldman

Paul Waldman is a weekly columnist and senior writer for the American Prospect. *He also writes for the Plum Line blog at the* Washington Post *and the* Week *and is the author of* Being Right Is Not Enough: What Progressives Must Learn From Conservative Success.

Everyone says we don't want new genetic engineering techniques to produce "designer babies." But would that be so bad?

Imagine you knew that you carried a gene for a debilitating illness. But doctors could go into your egg (or your spouse's) and remove that gene, enabling you to have a baby who, whatever other problems they might encounter through their lifetime, wouldn't have to worry about the illness. Would you let them? Most people would say probably yes, provided they were sure the technique was safe and wouldn't produce some kind of two-headed mutant centaur baby. That, after all, is what people were worried about when the first baby conceived via in-vitro fertilization was born in 1978—although in that case, they were worried about cyclops babies (seriously). It turned out in the end that IVF is perfectly safe, and now it's a common procedure, the ethics of which is questioned only by radical anti-choice extremists.

Well we may be approaching the time when doctors can fix certain kinds of inherited diseases before an egg is even fertilized. And naturally, people are worried about "designer babies," the phrase that gets repeated whenever the subject of this kind of genetic engineering comes up. This is a story from NPR yesterday:

"In Praise of Designer Babies," Paul Waldman, The American Prospect, October 10, 2013. Reprinted by permission.

The federal government is considering whether to allow scientists to take a controversial step: make changes in some of the genetic material in a woman's egg that would be passed down through generations.

Mark Sauer of the Columbia University Medical Center, a member of one of two teams of U.S. scientists pursuing the research, calls the effort to prevent infants from getting devastating genetic diseases "noble." Sauer says the groups are hoping "to cure disease and to help women delivery healthy normal children."

But the research also raises a variety of concerns, including worries it could open the door to creating "designer babies." The Food and Drug Administration has scheduled an Oct. 22 hearing to consider the issues.

There are legitimate concerns about safety, and just as with any new medical technique, those have to be thoroughly investigated before this kind of thing becomes common. But is a future of designer babies such a bad thing? I suspect it's one of those things we all assume would be terrible, but we seldom ask *why* it would be so bad.

So let's think about it for a moment. Unless you're a Christian Scientist, a religious sect most of us regard as deranged, no one says to the parents of a sick child, "Well, you just lost the luck of the draw there. It would be against nature to treat your child's illness." So why is it obvious that we should treat the illness after the child is born, but not prevent the illness beforehand?

Perhaps you're concerned about the slippery slope argument—we'll start treating awful diseases, but then quickly move to less critical medical needs, and on to purely elective procedures. But wouldn't the same logic apply? The fact that you might be able to convince a doctor to implant horns on your head isn't a very good argument for not letting a doctor use similar plastic surgery techniques to reconstruct a burn victim's nose. So why is it that we would say that the possibility of genetic engineering being used for something less urgent than preventing a life-threatening illness is a reason to not allow it to be used at all?

And it might be a very good thing to take a few steps down the slope. Genetic engineering of this type is in its infancy, but you could easily foresee a time when we could address all kinds of not life-threatening but still bothersome conditions. If we could free people from things on the order of allergies or myopia, that would be an enormous benefit to them.

One argument you're bound to hear is that technology like this will be distributed unequally, with the rich engineering their superbabies and the rest of of left to have run-of-the-mill children. That's certainly possible, but it depends on the cost of the intervention over the long term, and there's no way to tell yet how expensive it might be in 50 years. Right now we manage to distinguish between necessary medical procedures, which insurance will pay for, and elective ones, which are apportioned on the basis of wealth. Which means that rich people can have more symmetrical noses and perkier breasts and creepily unlined faces than ordinary people do, and that doesn't bother us enough to outlaw plastic surgery. You could envision a time when anyone can get their eggs adapted to remove a slate of harmful conditions and diseases, but only the rich can get the platinum service, which will also give your child shiny, manageable hair. We could probably tolerate that.

I do think we overestimate the degree to which genetic engineering could produce mass inequality. We already have lots of inequality based on genetics. Some people's parents are very smart and some people's parents are extraordinary athletes. Is it unfair that LeBron James' parents gave him the genes that made him six foot eight with loads of natural athletic talent? Not particularly. James himself didn't "deserve" his genetic lottery winnings any more than he would have if his parents were both 5 feet tall and had bought him the body he has through a medical intervention. Furthermore, you could make your next kid that tall, but there are a lot of other variables that would determine whether he actually became the world's best basketball player.

What about intelligence? If we could alter the genes in an egg or a sperm to make a child a bit smarter (which we are a long way from figuring out how to do, by the way), exactly what would be wrong with that? If you had a visceral reaction of opposition when you read that, ask yourself: Why? Try to articulate why it's wrong to use genetic engineering to make a child smarter than they might be if we were just flipping the genetic coin. "Because that's the way it's always been" isn't a persuasive answer. So what is it? Have we violated the free will of the child? Only if you think anyone would choose to be less intelligent than they are; and besides, parents violate their children's free will all the time. The child didn't ask to be smarter, but I didn't ask to have size 10 feet or bad vision; those decisions were made for me. The fact that it was a "natural" process that produced them doesn't make them any more a product of my will.

And it's hard to argue that as a society or a species we have too many smart people. What if a hundred years from now the technology had become safe, cheap, and easy, so a pregnant woman could pop a pill that costs a dollar and would boost her baby's IQ by 20 points—would you think it was wrong then? Keep in mind that parents already do a million things intended to help their developing children become healthier and smarter, some of which begin before the baby leaves the womb.

To repeat, there are serious and complex questions about how safe this kind of genetic engineering would be, and there is a real possibility of unforeseen consequences. But my point is that when we say, "We sure don't want designer babies" as though that's something everyone would naturally agree with, it's worth asking whether our instinctive reaction actually has a rational basis. I'm not a hundred percent sure that we want designer babies. But we might.

CHAPTER 2

Should We Be Afraid of Human Cloning?

Overview: Though Reproductive Cloning Has Ethical Issues, Therapeutic Cloning Shows Promise

Chamundeeswari Kuppuswamy, Darryl Macer, Mihaela Serbulea, and Brendan Tobin

Chamundeeswari Kuppuswamy, Darryl Macer, Mihaela Serbulea, and Brendan Tobin are former visiting research fellows at the United Nations University Institute for Advanced Studies.

Understanding Cloning

Cloning in essence means "making an exact copy." Cloning of cells is a commonplace procedure in the life sciences and reproductive cloning of some animals is now possible. Dolly the sheep was the first such mammal to be born, in 1997.[1] Although there has been some opposition to the cloning of mammals, by and large it has been generally accepted by society, however, it has brought the possibility of the cloning of human beings too close for comfort. While the majority of people do not support cloning of human beings, there are a small minority that do largely base their positions on issues of scientific freedom, reproductive rights and what some see as the inevitability that cloning will someday occur.[2]

Opponents have portrayed reproductive cloning as a violation of human dignity,[3] a position supported by the international community, in the Universal Declaration on the Human Genome and Human Rights (hereinafter "the Universal Declaration") which was unanimously adopted by all member states of UNESCO in their General Conference in November 1997, and unanimously endorsed by the General Assembly in 1998.[4] Article 11 of the Declaration states that "practices which are contrary to human dignity, such as reproductive cloning of human beings, shall not be permitted." Although the Universal Declaration is not a legally

Excerpt from "Is Human Reproductive Cloning Inevitable: Future Options for UN Governance," Chamundeeswari Kuppuswamy, Darryl Macer, Mihaela Serbulea, Brendan Tobin, United Nations University Institute of Advanced Studies, 2007.

binding instrument, it does provide ethical guidance that had global unanimity in 1997, and a number of countries have subsequently adopted legislation banning reproductive cloning.

The global community is split much more evenly with regard to debates over the way to govern scientific research using techniques of human cloning, which do not have the aim of reproduction. This split is in part due to ethical concerns but may also be due to a certain level of confusion over what this term means in practice, the scientific reasons for use of cloning techniques for medical research, and the actual relationship of such research to human reproductive cloning.[5]

While reproductive cloning is meant to result in an animal with the "exact" genetic imprint as the person whose cells are cloned, research cloning[6] is meant to produce tissues, which are an exact match to the person whose cells are cloned. There could be other uses for research cloning, as the name suggests.

Definition of Human Cloning

The Human Genome Organization (HUGO) defines "The term 'cloning,' while used in a general sense to refer to the production of genetic copies of individual organisms or cells without sexual reproduction, involves a number of different techniques, including embryo splitting; somatic cell nuclear transfer into an enucleated egg; and development of cell lines, derived from a somatic cell, in cell culture. Types of cloning may also be distinguished according to the organism in question and to the purpose for which the technique is employed. Human cloning, for example may be subdivided according to the purposes for which it is carried out reproductive cloning, basic research and therapeutic cloning."

The UNESCO/IUBS/Eubios Living Bioethics Dictionary[7] includes the following definitions:

CLONE: A collection of cells or organisms that are genetically identical. An identical genetic copy of an organism—animal/ plant/ human being.

CLONING: The process of asexually producing a group
of cells (clones), all genetically identical to the original
ancestor. In recombinant DNA manipulation procedures
to produce multiple copies of a single gene or segment
of DNA. The production of a cell or an organism from
a somatic cell of an organism with the same nuclear
genomic (genetic) characters—without fertilization.

REPRODUCTIVE CLONING: Use of CLONING
technology to produce one or more individuals genetically
identical (apart from the genes in MITOCHONDRIA
and CHLOROPLASTS) to another individual. In the
late 1990s reproductive cloning was used to produce
clones of the adults of a number of mammalian species,
including sheep, mice and pigs. The most famous of
these was DOLLY. Many countries rushed to outlaw
the possibility of reproductive cloning in humans. Most
bioethicists supported such bans though a minority were
more ambivalent.

THERAPEUTIC CLONING / RESEARCH CLONING:
Medical and scientific applications of cloning technology,
which do not result in the production of genetically
identical fetuses or babies.

EMBRYONIC STEM CELLS: (Anglo-Saxon stemm tree
or trunk & Latin *cella* storeroom). A formative cell whose
daughter cells give rise to other cell types; for example,
pluripotent embryonic stem cells are capable of generating
all cell types compared to the multipotent adult-derived
stem cells which generate many but not all cell types.
Thus, stem cells may originate from embryonic tissue and
from adult tissue and both types are suitable for cloning
technology; that is, therapeutic and/or reproductive.
Therapeutic cloning is the cloning of embryos containing
DNA from an individual's own cell to generate a source of
embryonic stem cell-progenitor cells that can differentiate

into the different cell types of the body. The aim is to produce healthy replacement tissue that would be readily available and due to immunocompatibility, the recipients would not have to take immunosuppressant drugs for the rest of their lives. The ethical status of embryonic stem cells is a matter of controversy because the label "embryo" is associated with cloning technology when typically embryonic stem cells are used. Strictly speaking, the early preimplantation blastocyst is not yet an embryo and is more properly called a pre-embryo. For this reason ethics commissions in several nations have approved research on the human pre-embryo up to 14 days because the conceptus is not yet differentiated. In this sense, the pre-embryo cells are no different from those in standard tissue cultures. On the other hand, it is true that a human pre-embryo could, in unscrupulous hands, be guided to develop into a human being. The protagonists against cloning maintain that by virtue of the pre-embryo's special status, it's wrong to carry out destructive experiments on them.

Reproductive Cloning

Reproductive cloning has been common place for some plants that we eat,[8] but it has been possible in animals for less than half a century. After the development of the technique of asexual reproduction of clonal frogs in the mid-1960s there was a period of much debate considering the possibility and ethics of cloning humans. However the 1950s and 1960s experiments in nuclear transfer in amphibians that could generate clones in some species could not be applied to mammals in scientific attempts at nuclear transfer from the 1960s until 1997. Robert Edwards, a pioneer of IVF, suggested in 1984 that making identical human twins could be useful in IVF as twin transfers give higher rates of implantation than single transfers. When it is only possible to obtain a single embryo from collecting eggs, it would increase the chances of a pregnancy if that embryo was split. Animal studies suggest this would present no extra harm to the babies born. In 1993 scientists reported experiments on splitting human embryos, and the growth of these "cloned twins." It has probably been technically possible for a decade. Most mammalian embryos can only be split into 2-4 clones, after that the cells lack the ability to start development into a human being.

In 1997 the paper in *Nature* reported the birth of the first cloned mammal from the transfer of an adult nucleus, "Dolly" the sheep.[9] This followed a paper the year before which made "Morag," the first cloned mammal, also a sheep, made by nuclear transfer from embryonic stem (ES) cells lines into an enucleated egg cell. Both sheep have since died and their stuffed bodies are displayed in the National Museum of Scotland, as symbols of scientific progress. On 24 November 2001 in Worcester, Mass, USA, a company reported in Scientific American "The First Human Cloned Embryo". It included cloned early-stage human embryos—and human embryos generated only from eggs, in a process called parthenogenesis (http://www.sciam. com/). In 2002-2003 the Raelian religious cult claimed that human cloned babies had been born, which is widely thought to be a publicity stunt. No scientific proof or baby has been presented.

Research Cloning

Research or therapeutic cloning as it is often referred to seeks to develop therapeutic remedies for degenerative diseases. This research requires the use of stem cells. Both embryonic and adult stem cells are being utilised in this research. Results from the use of adult stem cells have to date proved generally less favourable than those with embryonic stem cells. There is a general consensus that embryonic stem (ES) cells offer significantly more scientific chances of success than limiting research to adult cells. However, as discussed later, ES cells are controversial to use from an ethical point of view, hard to grow, hard to control (can become cancerous), are rejected in the body unless made to order for an individual by cloning or used in an immune protected site like the brain.

The preference of scientists to work with embryonic stem cells is at the root of research cloning activity which involves the development of embryos as a source of stem cells. This in turn has proved to be the catalyst for opposition to research cloning, opposition which is based on what is seen as the unethical an immoral development of embryo whose sole purpose is to provide stem cells.

In research that has subsequently been retracted, Woo Suk Hwang and colleagues of Seoul National University in Korea announced in the journal Science in February 2004[10] that they had successfully cloned healthy human embryos, removed embryonic stem cells and grown them in mice. This was the first claim that a human embryonic stem cell line could be made by research cloning in humans. They followed this up in May 2005 with claims of the successful cloning of stem cells from patients with Lou Gehrig disease, which showed proof of principle for the concept of making stem cells tailor-made to a patient for therapeutic ends.[11]

The 2004 findings were later shown to be fraudulent in one of the highest profile fraud cases of modern science. The media has been blamed as one of the causes for the widespread utopia that led many to argue for the need for embryonic stem cell research.[12] In spite of the continuous criticisms from bioethicists in Korea regarding the use of junior researchers as egg donors, Hwang was made a national hero and international star, fully supported by the government, mass media and people. Thanks to the information of a whistleblower and the tenacious investigation by the producers of MBC TV, his research was disclosed to be a huge fake. It was fortunate that the verification efforts of young scientists and prompt investigation by Seoul National University brought the case to conclusion. The Korean government hurriedly began to make a guideline for research ethics, and research integrity committees are appearing in many universities. The high profile case illustrates how a transparent research endeavour is necessary.[13]

There were, however, other cases reporting similar research results, but all have found it a major scientific challenge to improve success rates. There have also been reported to be some positive results from adult stem cell research with conversion of cells from one human organ into cells of another.[14] Others have restored normal function to rats whose spinal cords have been cut. Clinical trials using bone marrow to rebuild heart muscle have been successful. Regeneration of adult brain has been seen using adult cells in animals. There has also been a report of making liver cells from bone marrow of an adult—without cloning technology being needed.[15] Having said that, there is still a clear scientific consensus despite the Hwang case from the international community that research should be explored in ES lines because of the promising results to date. Support for ES research has been framed around a variety of themes, including freedom of scientific research, the expectation of medical benefits, and rights of patients to their dignity.

Resources

1. See generally Roslin Institute, http://www.ri.bbsrc.ac.uk/public/cloning.html
2. Amongst the arguments put forward in defence of cloning are those which argue that the cloned individual has a distinct personality, as in the case of identical twins. There are those also believe that human cloning is going to happen sooner or later. Others view a ban on cloning as a restriction of procreative liberty. The argument has also been raised that any impediment to cloning is an infringement of the human right to have children and a family. See Riordan, P.J., Cloning Consensus: Creating a Convention to ban human reproductive cloning, 26, Suffolk Transnat'l L.Rev.411 at 412, where he discusses the potential market and commercial application of the technology; Tully, P, Dollywood Is Not Just A Theme Park In Tennessee Anymore: Unwarranted Prohibitory Human Cloning Legislation And Policy Guidelines For A Regulatory Approach To Cloning, 31 J. Marshall L. Rev. 1385; Kunich Westport, J.C., The Naked Clone: How Cloning Bans Threaten Our Personal Rights, Praeger Publishers, 2003; Katz, K.D., The Clonal Child: Procreative Liberty and Asexual Reproduction, 8 Alb. L.J. Sci & Tech. 1, 40-51 (1997) Also see www.clonaid.com
3. Many scholars have a problem with viewing reproductive cloning as contrary to human dignity. See Caulfield, T., Human cloning laws, human dignity and the poverty of the policy making dialogue, BMC Medical Ethics 2003, 4:3 http://www.biomedcentral.com/1472-6939/4/3. The author argues that on most counts, autonomy, uniqueness, instrumentalisation and replication, reproductive cloning does not violate human dignity. He is of the view that we are in danger of trivializing and degrading the potential normative value of human dignity and

that unless we apply it in a logical and coherent fashion, the notion of human dignity is in danger of being eroded to the point where it stands as nothing more than a symbol of amorphous cultural anxiety. In Beyleveld D, Brownsword R: Human Dignity, Human Rights, and Human Genetics, The Modern Law Review 1998, 61:661-681, Beyleveld and Brownsword feel that "from any perspective that values rational debate about human genetics, it is an abuse of the concept of human dignity to operate it as a veto on any practice that is intuitively disliked." In Wright TG: Second Thoughts: How Human Cloning Can Promote Human Dignity, Valparaiso University Law Review 2000, the author argues against a deterministic conception of a human being and human dignity stating that "Human cloning may well serve to highlight, to emphasise, and to set off with greater clarity, quite apart from anyone's intentions, the mysterious capacities that comprise and express our human dignity." (Quoting from the Article by Caulfield, T.)

4. A/53/152
5. Box 1 lists several definitions of cloning
6. Research and Therapeutic cloning are used alternatively in this paper.
7. Available on website, http://eubios.info/biodict.htm
8. Asparagus is a common vegetable; Orchids are a common flower, reproduced by cloning. Many plants propagate vegetatively in nature, which is the same as cloning
9. Wilmut, I., et al. 1997. Viable offspring derived from fetal and adult mammalian cells. *Nature* 385 (Feb. 27):810
10. Woo Suk Hwang, et al, Evidence of a Pluripotent Human Embryonic Stem Cell Line Derived from a Cloned Blastocyst, Science 303, 1669 - 1674; 2004 (subsequently retracted)
11. Hwang, W. S.., Roh, S. I., Lee, B.C. et al (2005) "Patient-specific embryonic stem cells derived from human SCNT blastocysts," *Science*, 308: 1777-1783.
12. Karori Mbũgua, Stem Cell Research: Science, Ethics and the Popular Media, Stem Cell Research: Science, Ethics and the Popular Media, *EJAIB* 17 (2007), 6-11.
13. Solbakk, J.H. (2006) "Stem cell research and the ethics of transparency," *Regenerative Medicine* 1 (2006), 831-5.
14. Professor Jonathan Slack at Bath University has managed to convert human adult liver cells into pancreas cells producing insulin, using a simple chemical switch. *Nature Cell Biology*, 2, 879-887, 2000. , 2, 879-887, 2000.
15. May 15, 2002 *Journal of Clinical Investigation*. http://www.jci.org

All Human Cloning Must Be Banned

The US Department of State

The US Department of State directs the official position of the US in all international law.

UNITED STATES STATEMENT - 57 UNGA
SIXTH COMMITTEE Agenda Item 165.
International Convention Against the
Reproductive Cloning of HumanBeings.

Last year, the General Assembly established an Ad Hoc Committee of the Legal Committee to consider the issue of Human Cloning. The Committee met in February and, after hearing the views of a panel of scientists and bioethicists began discussion of the topic. A proposal was presented for a Convention which would prohibit the reproductive cloning of human beings. The United States took the position that a global and comprehensive ban is needed against creation of cloned human embryos for any purpose. President Bush elaborated on this position in addressing the issue in April 2002. The President said, "I believe all human cloning is wrong, and both forms of cloning ought to be banned. Anything other than a total ban on human cloning would be unethical. Research cloning would contradict the most fundamental principle of medical ethics, that no human life should be exploited or extinguished for the benefit of another."

In view of the preliminary discussions of the Ad Hoc Committee, which indicated a divergence of views on the proposal, the proponents of the convention to ban human reproductive cloning have slightly modified their proposal. They now suggest "a step-by-step" approach to these complex bioethical issues. First, there would be a ban on reproductive cloning of human beings. This could then lead, at a later stage, to "measures concerning the

"Views of the United States on Cloning," USUN, U.S. Department of State, September 23, 2002.

| 54

regulation of other types of cloning by interested States, including through the elaboration of a separate international instrument." They argue that such an approach would make it quite clear that a Convention against the reproductive cloning of human beings should not be seen as implicitly authorizing all types of cloning.

The United States does not agree. A ban that prohibited only "reproductive" cloning but did not address "therapeutic" or "experimental" cloning would implicitly authorize the creation and destruction of human embryos for experimentation. Furthermore, a ban on reproductive cloning would be impossible to enforce in an environment that permitted therapeutic cloning in laboratories. Once cloned embryos were available, it would be virtually impossible to control what was done with them, including the implantation of a cloned human embryo and bringing that embryo to term as a new cloned human. Indeed, even in the face of a ban on reproductive cloning, the scientist could export the cloned embryos to a jurisdiction where no such ban existed.

The proponents of a convention to ban human reproductive cloning have expressed concern that an attempt to achieve a ban on all types of cloning would undermine efforts to conclude a convention before a cloned human is produced. This view assumes that a convention could be negotiated and brought into force in a very short period. Recent conventions produced by the UN General Assembly have taken several years to enter into force. To ban "reproductive" cloning effectively, all human cloning must be banned. Under a partial ban that permitted the creation of cloned embryos for research, human embryos would be widely cloned in laboratories and assisted-reproduction facilities. Once cloned embryos were available, it would be virtually impossible to control what was done with them. Stockpiles of embryonic clones could be produced, bought and sold without anyone knowing it. Implantation of cloned embryos would take place out of sight, and even elaborate and intrusive regulations and policing would have great difficulty detecting or preventing the initiation of a clonal pregnancy. Once an illicit clonal pregnancy is begun, it would be virtually impossible to detect it. A ban only on "reproductive" cloning would therefore be a false ban, creating the illusion that such cloning had been prohibited. Furthermore, a completely effective ban would require universal acceptance to ensure that there were no safe havens for cloning activities.

It would be shortsighted to ignore the reality of this situation in the search for a solution through a step-by-step process, a process that would attempt to use two instruments, two regimes to deal with different aspects of a single problem, cloning, and which would take years to conclude. We must thwart this threat to human dignity through a total ban.

The United States, therefore, continues to support a ban on all human cloning and urges immediate action by the UN to put such a ban in place. We cannot agree to start down the road of a step-by-step process that would prohibit the production of cloned human beings but not prohibit the production of cloned human embryos for immediate destruction, an equal affront to human life and dignity.

In February the U.S. delegation presented a detailed description of the U.S. position. We would be pleased to provide copies of that paper to any delegation requesting it.

USUN September 23, 2002

The Views of the United States on the Science and Ethical Implications of Human Cloning

A. *The United States' Position*

The United States supports a global and comprehensive ban on human cloning through somatic cell nuclear transfer, regardless of the purpose for which the human clone is produced. The United States believes that so-called "therapeutic" or "experimental" cloning, which involves the creation and destruction of human embryos, must be part of this global and comprehensive ban. Thus, the Untied States does not support a ban that is limited merely to "reproductive" cloning.

Any ban on human cloning should explicitly state that it does not prohibit the use of nuclear transfer or other cloning techniques to produce DNA molecules, organs, plants, tissues, cells other than human embryos, or animals other than humans.

In addition, we believe that nations should actively pursue the potential medical and scientific benefits of adult stem-cell research. Such research does not require the exploitation and destruction of nascent human life, nor does it open the door to the dehumanizing possibilities that will come with the cloning of human beings.

B. Scientific Background

Cloning refers to any process that results in the creation of an identical or nearly identical genetic copy of a DNA molecule, cell, or individual plant, animal, or human. Cloning occurs in nature. For example, identical twins are the product of a natural cloning event. There have also been recent scientific developments in cloning, such as the 1997 live birth of a sheep created using an experimental cloning method called "somatic cell nuclear transfer."

Somatic cell nuclear transfer is a cloning technique used by scientists to produce a nearly genetically identical copy of an existing animal. The product of somatic cell nuclear transfer is an embryo. In simple terms, this embryo is created by replacing the nucleus of a female egg cell with genetic material from a "somatic" cell (which is a cell from the body other than a sperm or egg cell). There is no involvement of sperm. The resulting embryo is a clone that is nearly genetically identical to the donor of the somatic cell. (Since the donor egg also contains non-nuclear DNA in subcellular structures called mitochondria, the clone's cells contain a very small amount of mitochondrial DNA from the donor egg cell. Thus, the clone is not exactly genetically identical to the somatic cell donor.)

Scientists conduct two types of experiments using somatic cell nuclear transfer. The first type of experiment, sometimes described as "reproductive" cloning, involves the creation of an embryo through cloning, and its subsequent implantation into the uterus with the objective of creating a living animal. Animal reproductive cloning experiments have very high failure rates (around 95%) and often result in stillbirths, spontaneous abortions, or offspring with severe congenital abnormalities.

The other kind of experiment, sometimes described as "research," "experimental," or "therapeutic" cloning, involves the creation of a cloned embryo, which is then used to derive stem cells or (after the embryo is grown to a fetal stage) tissues for transplantation. For example, after the embryo grows to the blastocyst stage (5-9 days), the embryo is destroyed in order to derive embryonic stem cells that may hold the potential for the development of cell replacement therapies. (Stem cells are discussed more fully in the attachment.) Hypothetically, therapies based on stem cells derived from cloned human embryos would not be subject to immune rejection if transplanted into the human donor of the somatic cell used for cloning. Other kinds of research on cloned embryos have also been attempted. Recently, researchers have reported that they have grown cloned animal embryos in an animal host uterus beyond the blastocyst stage and successfully extracted differentiated tissue for replacement therapy.

Whatever its purpose, cloning through human somatic cell nuclear transfer necessarily involves the creation of a living human embryo. For this reason, the technique raises profound ethical and moral questions and is highly controversial.

There are other cloning techniques that do not raise these moral and ethical concerns. For example, scientists routinely employ cellular or molecular cloning in their work to make genetically identical cells for research. Although these other cloning techniques could be used to develop therapies to treat disease, scientists do not use the term "therapeutic" to describe these techniques. Rather, as discussed above, the term "therapeutic" cloning is used by scientists to describe cloning by somatic cell nuclear transfer for therapeutic, as opposed to reproductive, purposes. This latter type of cloning is also described as "experimental" cloning, or "cloning for research purposes."

C. Ethical Implications of a Partial Ban on Human Cloning

Human cloning—for any purpose—is an enormously troubling development in biotechnology. It is unethical in itself and dangerous as a precedent.

The possible creation of a human being through cloning raises many ethical concerns. It constitutes unethical experimentation on a child-to-be, subjecting him or her to enormous risks of bodily and developmental abnormalities. It threatens human individuality, deliberately saddling the clone with the genetic makeup of a person who has already lived. It risks making women's bodies a commodity, with women being paid to undergo risky drug treatment so they will produce the many eggs that are needed for cloning. It is also a giant step toward a society in which life is created for convenience, human beings are grown for spare body parts, and children are engineered to fit eugenic specification.

We cannot allow human life to be devalued in this way. A proposal has been made to ban only so-called "reproductive" cloning, by prohibiting the transfer of a cloned embryo into a woman to begin a pregnancy in the hopes of creating a human baby. This approach is unsound.

First, a ban that prohibited only "reproductive" cloning, but left "therapeutic" or "experimental" cloning unaddressed, would essentially authorize the creation and destruction of human embryos explicitly and solely for research and experimentation. It would turn nascent human life into a natural resource to be mined and exploited, eroding the sense of the worth and dignity of the individual. This prospect is repugnant to many people, including those who do not believe that the embryo is a "person."

Second, to ban "reproductive" cloning effectively, *all* human cloning must be banned. Under a partial ban that permitted the creation of cloned embryos for research, human embryos would be widely cloned in laboratories and assisted-reproduction facilities. Once cloned embryos are available, it would be virtually impossible to control what was done with them. Stockpiles of embryonic clones could be produced, bought and sold without anyone knowing it.

Implantation of cloned embryos, an easy procedure, would take place out of sight, and even elaborate and intrusive regulations and policing could not detect or prevent the initiation of a clonal pregnancy. Once begun, an illicit clonal pregnancy would be virtually impossible to detect. And if detected, governments would be unlikely to compel the pregnancy to be aborted or severely penalize the pregnant woman for allowing the implantation or for failure to abort the pregnancy. A ban only on "reproductive" cloning would therefore be a false ban, creating the illusion that such cloning had been prohibited.

Third, a ban that permits embryonic clones to be created and forbids them to be implanted in utero legally *requires* the destruction of nascent human life and criminalizes efforts to preserve and protect it once created, a morally abhorrent prospect.

Fourth, there may be other routes to solving the transplant rejection problems, and there is to date no animal research to support the claim that cloned embryonic stem cells are therapeutically efficacious. A legal ban on "therapeutic" cloning would allow time for the investigation of promising and less problematic research alternatives such as "adult" stem-cell research. It would also allow time for policy makers and the public to develop more informed judgments about cloning, and for the establishment of regulatory structures to oversee applications of cloning technology that society deems acceptable.

There are other cloning techniques that do not raise these moral and ethical concerns. For example, scientists routinely employ cellular or molecular cloning in their work to make genetically identical cells for research. These other cloning techniques—that do not entail the creation and destruction of human embryos—are currently being used to develop therapies to treat disease. Any ban on human cloning should explicitly state that it does not prohibit the use of nuclear transfer or other cloning techniques to produce molecules, organs, plants, tissues, cells other than human embryos, or animals other than humans.

We believe that States should actively pursue the potential medical and scientific benefits of adult stem-cell research. Such research does not require the exploitation and destruction of nascent human life, nor does it open the door to the dehumanizing possibilities that will come with the cloning of human beings.

The United States does not support a ban limited to "reproductive" cloning. We believe that so-called "therapeutic" or "experimental" cloning, which involves the creation and destruction of human embryos, must be included.

Thus, the United States supports a global and comprehensive ban on human cloning through somatic cell nuclear transfer, regardless of the purpose for which the human clone is produced. We look forward to working with other delegations to achieve that objective.

Attachment: Stem Cell Overview

Cloned human embryos produced through somatic cell nuclear transfer are potentially a source of human embryonic stem cells. They could also be used for other experimental purposes. This attachment provides some information about embryonic and adult stem cells.

Stem cells are cells that occur in animals at all stages of development, front the embryo to the adult. They have different properties and abilities, depending on the age of the organism and the location of the stem cells within the organism.

Embryonic stem cells are derived from a 5-9 day-old embryo and are able to generate nearly all the cell types of the body. To date, human embryonic stem cell research has been conducted using stem cells derived from embryos that were created in the course of in vitro fertilization and were no longer needed for that purpose.

Adult stem cells occur in small numbers throughout the bodies of adult mammals. Under normal conditions, they generate the cell types of the tissue in which they reside. Under certain experimental conditions in the laboratory, or even after transplant into a living animal, adult stem cells may be able to differentiate into the specialized cells of several different tissues.

All stem cells are unspecialized (undifferentiated)—they do not have any specific structures that allow them to perform specific functions such as carry oxygen or fire an electrical signal. Unlike specialized cells such as muscle cells, blood cells, or nerve cells, which divide slowly or not at all, stem cells are also capable of dividing and renewing themselves for long periods (self-renewing). Importantly, stem cells retain the unique ability to give rise to specialized cells (differentiation), such as muscle, skin, or neurons.

Scientists believe that human stem cells—embryonic and adult, differentiated to specific cell types—offer the possibility of a renewable source of replacement cells and tissues to treat a myriad of diseases.

Human Cloning Crosses Numerous Ethical Boundaries

Sophia M. Kolehmainen, JD

Sophia Kolehmainen, JD, MSEL, is the Human Genetics Program Director for the Council for Responsible Genetics ("CRG"). CRG is a national nonprofit organization made up of scientists, lawyers, academics, and concerned citizens dedicated to broadening the debate about the use of the new genetic technologies. The organization is based in Cambridge, Massachusetts, and focuses on two main program areas: commercial biotechnology and the environment and human genetics.

Introduction

Until recently, discussions about human cloning were conducted within the realm of science fiction and fantasy. However, with the successful cloning of the sheep "Dolly" in 1997, it became evident that sooner or later, scientists might be able to clone human beings, too. This possibility has incited both support and opposition. Newspapers and magazines have described cloning as an exciting step forward that allows genetic engineers to reduce the uncertainties of reproduction, but they have also published commentaries by scientists, religious figures, and others who see human cloning as an attack on human dignity. This Essay focuses on whether we as a society should accept human cloning by somatic cell nuclear transfer to create offspring.

Cloning: The Science of Controversy

Somatic cell nuclear transfer is the cloning technique that was used by the Scottish scientists to produce Dolly. It involves the removal of DNA from an egg-cell and fusion of that enucleated

"Human Cloning: Brave New Mistake," by Sophia M. Kolehmainen, Council for Responsible Genetics. Reprinted by permission.

egg with a differentiated cell from an already existing organism, like a skin cell, or in the case of Dolly, a mammary cell from a sheep which had been dead for six years. The Scottish scientists found that fusing the two cells with an electric shock triggered a "reprogramming" which caused the combined egg-mammary cell to divide and mature like an early embryo.

Cloning technology developed as a way to improve the production of genetically engineered animals. There are huge financial profits to be made by developing genetically engineered animals that secrete chemicals and proteins of value to humans, such as cows or goats that produce human blood clotting agents in their milk. Without cloning, scientists must genetically manipulate each individual animal, which results in very low success rates. However, with cloning comes the possibility that scientists need only perfect one animal to clone an entire herd from that success. The goal is not to copy everything about the animal, only the property that has been engineered into it. The desire of some genetic engineers to gain control over the innermost workings of animals fueled the further development of cloning technology. It is out of this context that some people are now attempting to justify human cloning.

The transfer of cloning techniques to humans, however, creates a host of unique technical, ethical and social issues that aren't currently raised in the cloning of animals. Whereas the point of cloning animals is to create more economically efficient bio-factories of identical animals with value to humans, cloning humans is being suggested as a procreative technique to copy existing people.

In 1998 reporters covered Richard Seed's declaration that he intended to raise the funds to produce two to three copies of himself through cloning. This announcement illustrates the false view held by many that cloning will result in exact copies of existing, or dead, individuals. This is just not true. The cloning process would never produce an exact copy of the cloned person. Though an individual manufactured by cloning would posses the same genetic sequence as the person whose nucleus was used other factors also substantially affect the development of an individual. An individual's development may be affected by structural and metabolic influences of the enucleated egg and the differentiated cell, as well as influences during gestation. In addition, non-genetic factors such as nutrition, home environment, education, economic situation, and culture add significantly to the development of personhood. Just as with animals, cloning humans will never produce exact copies.

Other false views persist in the language of cloning, namely equating cloning with reproduction, and equating cloning with the birth of identical twins. A cloned individual would be one made by scientists, using a pre-existing genetic configuration, without the joining of gametes from two people. The cloning process is not sexual reproduction, but is more akin to asexual replication of organisms that simply split in two. The production of a clone is vastly different from the process by which twins are born. So-called identical twins, though genetically identical to one another, have two genetic parents, and are still biologically unprecedented in that their genetic configuration has never existed before.

Brave New Mistake

It would be a mistake to develop and use cloning as a technique to replicate human beings. It is questionable what benefits would be gained from the successful creation of a cloned human being, if any, and whether they would justify the radical impact cloning would have on our society. Cloning is not just another reproductive technology that should be made available to those who choose to use it, but is an unnecessary and dangerous departure from evolutionary processes and social practices that have developed over millions of years. As with many other developments in biotechnology, some scientists and commentators are asking us to accept cloning of humans just because it is technically possible, but there are few good reasons to develop the technology, and many reasons not to develop it.

1. Safety Concerns

The most frequently stated argument against cloning is based on safety concerns. After the news of Dolly, President Clinton convened the National Bioethics Advisory Commission (NBAC) to review the legal and ethical issues of the potential cloning of a human. The NBAC heard testimony and read opinions on the multitude of complex issues surrounding human cloning, but in the end, the NBAC based its recommendation for a three to five year moratorium on human cloning in the United States on safety concerns.

At this point in the process of experimenting with cloning, safety is an important concern. The production of Dolly required at least 276 failed attempts. No one knows why these attempts failed and why one succeeded. Cloning presents different obstacles in every species, as embryo implantation, development, and gestation differ among different species. Human cloning therefore could not become a reality without extensive human experimentation. Though 276 "failed" lambs may be acceptable losses, the ethical implications of failed or partially successful human experiments are unacceptable.

Inhibitions concerning human experimentation would seem to be an impassable ethical and practical barrier to human cloning, but there may come a time when scientists feel they have enough knowledge from animal experiments to proceed with human trials. Even if questions of safety could be eliminated, which is highly unlikely, or if public opinion and scientific hubris were to reach the point where the risks associated with human experimentation seemed less egregious, human cloning should still be prohibited for several reasons.

2. Commodification

Cloning would encourage the commodification of humans. Though industrialized societies commodify human labor and human lives, the biological commodification involved in human cloning would be of a vastly different order. Cloning would turn procreation into a manufacturing process, where human characteristics become added options and children, objects of deliberate design. This process of commodification needs to be actively opposed. It produces no benefits and it undermines the very basis of our established notions of human individuality and dignity.

3. Human Diversity
Cloning would also disrespect human diversity in ethnicity and ability. Though it is not possible to produce exact copies of animals or people, inherent in cloning is the desire to do so. The process of cloning would necessarily increase conformity, and eradicate genetic variety. A society that supported cloning as an acceptable procreative technique, would imply that variety is not important. Especially in a multicultural nation like the United States, where diversity and difference are of the essence, any procedure that reduced our acceptance of differences would be dangerous. It is clear from the tensions that exist in our society that we should be embracing processes that increase our appreciation for the diversity of individuals, not working to remove differences.

4. Permanent Changes to the Gene Pool
The process of cloning would inevitably invite the use of other genetic technologies, specifically genetic manipulation of cloned embryos, and this could result in permanent, heritable changes to the human gene pool. Some scientists pretend that they can predict which genes humans would be better off without. However, there is no way to acquire the requisite genetic knowledge to make such a prediction without experimental genetic manipulation, which would have implications for subsequent generations. Such experiments must not be done, since both the errors and supposed successes of genetic manipulation would be with humanity forever. Although the potential applications of human genetic engineering may appeal to some, the experimental nature of the technique, and the permanence of the results, would make it a highly dangerous innovation.

5. Threat of Eugenics

Cloning would allow for genetic manipulation that sets the stage for increased efforts at eugenics. Eugenics is the attempt to improve human beings, not by improving their economic, social, and educational opportunities, but by altering the genes with which they are born. Cloning would allow scientists to begin with a known human prototype (the person to be cloned) and then "improve" it by modifying specific traits. People who wanted to be cloned could have themselves cloned only to be taller, blonder, smarter. The threat of eugenics is inherent in technologies that allow individuals to try to modify inherited characteristics so as to give preference to specific ones. It would be impossible to embark on human cloning without opening the door to eugenics. After all, cloning in animals by "improving" their inherited characteristics is a deliberate form of animal eugenics.

6. Natural Procreation and Evolution

Ordinary procreation, whether it results in twins or singletons, is an open-ended process that depends on the random coming together of an egg and sperm cell. Each new individual has a unique configuration of genes which leads to an amazing range of human variability. Cloning forecloses the opportunity for genetic surprise and growth among cloned humans, limiting such future people to genetic configurations that have been expressed before.

Cloning Is Not a Reproductive Answer

The discussion above provides a strong basis to support a prohibition on human cloning. Cloning developed in the context of animal commodification and the technique's intent and purposes are not applicable in humans. Even setting aside the fact that cloning cannot produce exact copies, and that it cannot go forward without much prior human experiment, the above arguments weigh heavily against ever allowing the cloning of humans.

In addition, there are no clear, defensible arguments in favor of offering cloning as an option for producing offspring. Cloning is endorsed by some as a procreative technique that provides a cure to infertility or an option for people who have genes they do not want to pass on and the chance to have genetically related offspring for gay and lesbian couples or people without partners. Such arguments are not convincing.

Their flaws stem from the fallacy of their premise and their neglect of the availability of other, less questionable, options. First, if cloning were in fact a "cure" for infertility, then infertility would no longer exist. Newborns, elderly people, women who have had complete hysterectomies, and people born without ovaries or testes would all be able to bear offspring. In reality, cloning does nothing to alleviate the underlying environmental or social causes of infertility. Labeling cloning as a cure for infertility implies the acceptance of entirely new definitions of fertility and infertility, and is therefore misleading. Technically, cloning is replication of that which already exists. It is not a "cure" for anything.

Current reproductive technologies offer couples who have genes they don't want to pass on, or gays, lesbians, and people without partners an array of alternatives to cloning. People can choose genetic testing to avoid transmitting certain genes to their offspring. Lesbians, gays, and unpartnered people can acquire sperm, eggs, embryos and gestational ("surrogate") mothers. Adoption is another option.

Problems associated with rising rates of infertility will not be solved through the development of high-tech, invasive and expensive interventions. Even now, rather than answering the needs of people unable to reproduce, many of the new technologies used in assisted reproduction actually create needs and make it increasingly difficult for people to accept other, less complex and invasive solutions. The psychological problems associated with infertility are created by societal as well as by personal pressures, and should be understood and dealt with at that level.

Some proponents of human cloning who recognize the weakness of their arguments, continue to support the development of human cloning under the banner of freedom—freedom of reproductive choice and freedom of scientific inquiry. They argue that people should have the choice to produce offspring in this way, and scientists should have the option to explore human cloning without outside interference. With these arguments, proponents of human cloning are able to side-step the lack of clear benefits of this technology by raising a banner to "freedom" and "choice."

The ill-defined boundaries of a person's right to procreative autonomy makes some people cautious about prohibiting cloning. The NBAC report noted that a prohibition on cloning would be in tension with the fundamental right to procreate. The right to privacy and some level of autonomy in decision-making about procreation can be traced through a series of Supreme Court decisions. Generally speaking, this line of cases supports the notion that the decision whether to bear or not to bear a child is one which is of the most personal and private nature and should therefore be made without governmental interference. Some cloning proponents have extended this right to mean that the government has an obligation to support the development of all techniques that may help citizens reproduce.

This is an improper expansion of the right to be free from governmental interference in reproductive decision-making. A prohibition on cloning does not interfere with that right because the government does not have the obligation to ensure that each citizen who wants a child has a child. The right covers only the right of individuals, who can reproduce, to reproduce (or not) without government interference. Providing and safe-guarding the option to clone, in the face of the numerous negative implications of the technology, is not an acceptable justification to support the technique.

Another argument used to counter a prohibition on cloning is that it would stifle scientific inquiry. But, science is not an unbiased, objective field of study, and not all scientific possibilities need be accepted by society. Scientific research is conducted by people with personal and professional interests in the outcome and continuation of their work. It is often motivated by a quest for profits and power. A prohibition on human cloning may indeed make it more difficult for scientists to study some inherited genetic diseases, though that is far from clear. However, allowing cloning in order to meet this hypothetical need would radically alter our current concepts of humanity and of procreation. Not all scientific inquiry has equal priority and the question should be who gets to set the priorities; scientists, their funders, or the public. Like other publicly supported activities, science must serve the public interest and the public should have the power to influence decisions about which paths are worth exploring.

Cloning

The cloning debate, like the debates surrounding the introduction of many of the new genetic technologies, often reflects the proposition that if science can do something, it should be done. Scientists introduce new technologies with inflated promises of potentially solving the world's problems—genetically engineered crops to end world hunger, or mapping the human genome so as to end disease. Researchers and their investors promote these technologies without proof of actual benefit or lack of harm. In reality, many of these "miracle" inventions could cause harm, and to date few of the promised benefits have been realized.

Human cloning represents another one of these false "miracles." It would cure no disease while it would markedly alter our relationships to each other and the natural world. Human cloning cannot proceed without crossing numerous ethical boundaries. With no identifiable benefit to the technique, existing social and legal arguments against it should not be set aside, and human cloning should therefore be permanently banned.

Human Cloning Should Be Embraced

Russell Blackford

Russell Blackford is conjoint lecturer in philosophy at the University of Newcastle, Australia. Blackford is a fellow with the Institute for Ethics and Emerging Technologies, a laureate of the International Academy of Humanism, and editor-in-chief of the Journal of Evolution and Technology.

D olly, the world's most famous and controversial sheep, was born twenty years ago—on July 5, 1996 to be precise. She was the first mammal to enter the world following a process of reproductive cloning, making the event a spectacular scientific breakthrough.

To create Dolly, researchers at the Roslin Institute in Scotland employed a technique known as somatic cell nuclear transfer (SCNT). With SCNT, DNA from the nucleus of an ordinary cell—obtained from anywhere in an animal's body—is transferred into an enucleated oocyte (egg cell), typically from a different animal.

In Dolly's case, her DNA came from one sheep's mammary cell; it was implanted into an egg from another sheep; and the resulting tiny biological entity was implanted into the uterus of yet a third sheep, where it grew until birth.

The result of SCNT is a creature with almost the same genetic potential as the one providing the nuclear DNA. SCNT is thus a powerful, and often effective, form of animal cloning.

Dolly is born! Announcement and reaction

Subsequently, in February 1997, Ian (now Sir Ian) Wilmut and his research team at the Roslin Institute announced Dolly's birth in the prestigious science journal *Nature*. This provoked political and ethical debates that have never truly stopped.

Public discussion of cloning gradually receded in prominence as new issues arose to dominate the airwaves and the headlines, notably the threat of jihadist terrorism following the attacks on September 11, 2001. But issues relating to cloning technology remain crucial to debates over biomedical research and its regulation.

The announcement—with a description of the method used to bring Dolly into existence—triggered a feverish worldwide response because of the possible implications for human cloning. It was immediately obvious that SCNT could, in principle, be used to create human babies. Across the world, many countries banned human cloning—often with significant punishments, such as lengthy jail terms, even for attempting such a thing.

The case against cloning

The actual arguments against human cloning are extremely varied, and I cannot elaborate them all here. (I go into more of them, and in far more depth, in my 2014 book, *Humanity Enhanced: Genetic Choice and the Challenge for Liberal Democracies*).

One common claim is that bringing children into the world in this way is somehow a violation of the natural order, or of human dignity; or perhaps it would be an act of "playing God." Unfortunately, it can be very difficult to pin down precisely what any of these claims really mean in the context of bioethical debate. I am, for example, sceptical about the existence of anything that can correctly be called "human dignity."

Some critics fear that children created via SCNT would be subjected to unfair expectations of duplicating the talents and achievements of whoever provided their nuclear DNA. Sometimes the critics speak in terms of the autonomy of the child being violated, diminished or denied, although it can be very difficult to spell out exactly what this amounts to. In *Humanity Enhanced*, I challenge the idea that children conceived through SCNT would have their autonomy violated—or would somehow lack or lose autonomy—in any sense inapplicable to "ordinary" children.

Some critics worry about a larger social effect, or even an effect on our species, if cloning restricted the diversity of children being born (perhaps because parents and doctors might look for donors with a narrow range of characteristics, such as possessing high intelligence and meeting certain standards of physical beauty).

Yet other arguments acknowledge that reproductive cloning in itself might not have a great social or species-wide impact; however, it's claimed, cloning could place human societies on a slippery slope toward accepting even more radical technological interventions such as genetic engineering of human traits. On one version of the approach, this would, in turn, set us upon a path to unequivocally horrible social outcomes. Thus cloning supposedly confronts us with a slippery slope to another slippery slope … which seems like a tenuous style of argument.

Though some of these fears may have an element of truth, they are all exaggerated. In my view, which I've defended in *Humanity Enhanced* and other publications, human cloning would not be a seriously worrying action if we could carry it out safely.

To some extent, however, all of this is moot. Over the past twenty years, we have enjoyed success in cloning many mammalian species, but no one has cloned a human being. Indeed, we have been frustrated in efforts to clone other primates such as apes and monkeys.

In the upshot, human reproductive cloning is not yet feasible, and indeed there's no current prospect that it could be carried out effectively and safely in the foreseeable future. Even if we did conceive a human embryo through SCNT, and we then managed to bring it to term, the odds are very high that the result would be a seriously deformed child.

That's a good pragmatic reason not to make attempts until we know a lot more, and even then we'd need to have developed the technology to a point where we are about as likely as with ordinary births to end up with a healthy baby.

I don't rule out that someone might accomplish this technological feat one day, but, once again, there is no sign of it happening. Nor is it what SCNT research is really about from the point of view of reputable medical researchers. The real action is with what is known as "therapeutic cloning." Allow me to explain.

Reproductive and therapeutic cloning

So far I've focused on "reproductive cloning," and more specifically on human reproductive cloning: the postulated use of SCNT (or any other technique that might have a similar result) to bring about the birth of a human child.

By contrast, the expression "therapeutic cloning" refers to the creation of human embryos by SCNT for some other purpose, such as for biomedical research or for harvesting cells or tissues to be used in therapies.

Although some ethical issues are raised with therapeutic cloning—including a concern that the associated research destroys human embryos—the idea has been obtaining legal acceptance in some countries, usually subject to tight government regulation. If we start to see impressive results from therapeutic cloning, with new therapies emerging from the research, I expect that it will eventually obtain the same wide acceptance that IVF—in vitrofertilization—now enjoys in Western countries. (It's not that long ago that IVF was also widely regarded as abhorrent.)

More generally, people come to embrace new technologies, even those that initially seemed shocking and "unnatural," once concrete benefits become clear.

Twenty years later

Two decades later, I'm not sure that the ethical arguments advanced for and against human cloning are greatly different from those we saw back 1997. However, the early debate was very one-sided. The initial response to the dramatic *Nature* article by Wilmut et al. was largely one of fear, mingled with disgust, with too little rational reflection. Since then, the fear-mongering has partly died down, but not before a great deal of draconian legislation was enacted across the world. Little chance was given for calmer voices—or any dissenting voices—to be heard before governments took action.

As it seems to me, calmer voices eventually won the academic debate. There is a strong sense, within the field of secular bioethics, that the early arguments against human reproductive and therapeutic cloning were flawed. However, dissenters lost the politicaldebate almost before it began. Politicians, journalists, many academics, and the general public in our Western liberal democracies greeted the very idea of human cloning with a cascade of hostility.

The expressions of fear, disgust, and moral outrage appeared immediately; in response, highly illiberal laws were enacted without due consideration of the issues.

But more reasonable people are slowly winning back the central political ground, gradually making the public case that technologies based on SCNT may bring many benefits. That, perhaps, will be the story of the next twenty years.

Human Cloning Offers Medical Benefits

Jayashree Pakhare

Jayashree Pakhare is a science writer and teacher.

The process of creation of genetically identical person from either a living or dead person is known as human cloning. It includes the production of clone tissues, also donated from the individual to be cloned. This term refers to artificial human cloning only. The birth of twins is called natural human cloning. Even though the birth of twins is the result of natural human cloning they are separate people with separate experience. The presence of identical DNA makes no difference in their being different personalities. The scientific community all over the world is still investigating the question how similar the original and its clone would be and this may depend up on how much of personality traits are determined by genes. Scientists have managed to clone animals like Dolly, the sheep. They have obviously tried the same method on humans, and have reached considerable success. However, many countries and governments have banned human cloning fearing the ill-effects of human clones. The human race is not yet prepared to come face-to-face with clones moving about with normal people. There is a huge debate on the pros and cons of human cloning. This Buzzle article on human cloning will cover the advantages of cloning humans.

Techniques of Human Cloning and Claim of Success

The most common technique used in human cloning is "somatic cell nuclear transfer." Under this technique, the nucleus of an egg cell taken from a donor is removed. Then, the original cell gets fused with another cell of same genetic material to be cloned.

"Human Cloning Benefits," Buzzle, Reprinted by permission.

Another technique used, is parthenogenesis. This technique involves inducement of unfertilized egg to divide and grow as if it were fertilized. As recently as on May 2005, a team of scientists led by Mr Hwang Woo-Suk attached to Seoul National University, claimed to have created 11 lines of human stem cells using a different technique. [This claim was later determined to be fraudulent.]

Benefits of Human Cloning

There are some ways by which human cloning can benefit the humankind. Here is a list of advantages.

Cloning People

One of the main reasons why human cloning turns out to be a scary affair, is that it would allow people to clone themselves. Just imagine, you could get a twin by cloning yourself. Parents who lose their children to death may get tempted to clone their dead child. Some may think of cloning Einstein or Usain Bolt and give rise to a league of superhumans or super-sportsmen. Those against humanity may give rise to clones of the famous villains in of our history. Although the idea of a clone sounds pretty attractive, no one knows how the clone will behave and will he/she develop similar personalities like its master clone.

Rejuvenation

It has been found that the production of clone tissue should be helpful in making aging people look young. According to Dr. Richard Seed, one of the leading proponents of human cloning technology, one day it should be possible to reverse the aging process.

Heart Attack Treatment

Today, heart attack is the number one killer in the developed as well as developing countries. Scientists believe that by cloning healthy heart cells and injecting them in to the damaged heart area, they can treat heart attacks.

Human stem cells

It has been experimented that nascent cells can be grown to produce human organs or tissues. This can be used for repairing or replacing the damaged organs. A combination of human stem cells production and human cloning technology can be used to produce tissues for suffering people, which are otherwise rejected by their immune system.

Infertility treatment

The success rate of current infertility treatments is very low. Further, the couple has to go through tormenting procedures with a small chance of getting a child. The advent of cloning technology will make it possible for infertile couples to have [children more] than ever before.

Use in Surgeries

Presently silicon gels and other cosmetics are being used in surgery. These materials not only suit the patients but also cause immune disease. In human cloning, doctors, instead of using materials foreign to the body are able to grow cells, bones, tissues that match that of person taking treatment. Victims of terrible accidents with deformed faces can hope to have their features repaired with safe technology. The case of breast implants for cosmetic reasons is also similar. With the silicone implants, people developed illness of their immune system.

Defective genes

It is estimated that an average person has 8 defective genes inside him. People with defective genes will develop illness in spite of their keeping good health otherwise. With cloning, it is possible to have genes without any defects.

Other benefits

By switching cells on and off through cloning, it has been found that cancer can be cured. The phenomenon of cells differentiating into specific kinds of tissue was baffling the scientists. Cloning may hold the key in making them understand differentiation and cancer. Down's syndrome, liver failure, kidney failure, leukemia, spinal cord injury, genetic diseases are some of the ailments which can also be cured by cloning.

The success stories of human cloning and creating tissue cells have come from different parts of the world. People have also been treated with the technology and have started to realize some benefits of cloning. The response and feedback the Human Cloning Foundation has been getting is a testament of the popularity this form of science is getting all over the world. But, many countries have not accepted this. The human cloning has not been given legal status in many countries. However, the stem cell research has been accepted by some governments. Till the scientific community comes up with a legally acceptable human clone, God, the creator of all human beings, born and to be born, can continue to enjoy, the status of a "creative maverick"!

CHAPTER 3

Is Genetically Modified Food Good for the World?

Overview: The Safety of Genetically Modified Food Continues to Be Assessed and Debated

World Health Organization

The World Health Organization directs and coordinates international health within the United Nations' system.

Frequently asked questions on genetically modified foods

These questions and answers have been prepared by WHO in response to questions and concerns from WHO Member State Governments with regard to the nature and safety of genetically modified food.

1. What are genetically modified (GM) organisms and GM foods?

Genetically modified organisms (GMOs) can be defined as organisms (i.e. plants, animals or microorganisms) in which the genetic material (DNA) has been altered in a way that does not occur naturally by mating and/or natural recombination. The technology is often called "modern biotechnology" or "gene technology," sometimes also "recombinant DNA technology" or "genetic engineering." It allows selected individual genes to be transferred from one organism into another, also between nonrelated species. Foods produced from or using GM organisms are often referred to as GM foods.

2. Why are GM foods produced?

GM foods are developed—and marketed—because there is some perceived advantage either to the producer or consumer of these foods. This is meant to translate into a product with a lower price, greater benefit (in terms of durability or nutritional value) or both.

"Frequently asked questions on genetically modified foods," World Health Organization. Reprinted by permission.

Initially GM seed developers wanted their products to be accepted by producers and have concentrated on innovations that bring direct benefit to farmers (and the food industry generally).

One of the objectives for developing plants based on GM organisms is to improve crop protection. The GM crops currently on the market are mainly aimed at an increased level of crop protection through the introduction of resistance against plant diseases caused by insects or viruses or through increased tolerance towards herbicides.

Resistance against insects is achieved by incorporating into the food plant the gene for toxin production from the bacterium Bacillus thuringiensis (Bt). This toxin is currently used as a conventional insecticide in agriculture and is safe for human consumption. GM crops that inherently produce this toxin have been shown to require lower quantities of insecticides in specific situations, e.g. where pest pressure is high. Virus resistance is achieved through the introduction of a gene from certain viruses which cause disease in plants. Virus resistance makes plants less susceptible to diseases caused by such viruses, resulting in higher crop yields.

Herbicide tolerance is achieved through the introduction of a gene from a bacterium conveying resistance to some herbicides. In situations where weed pressure is high, the use of such crops has resulted in a reduction in the quantity of the herbicides used.

3. Is the safety of GM foods assessed differently from conventional foods?

Generally consumers consider that conventional foods (that have an established record of safe consumption over the history) are safe. Whenever novel varieties of organisms for food use are developed using the traditional breeding methods that had existed before the introduction of gene technology, some of the characteristics of organisms may be altered, either in a positive or a negative way. National food authorities may be called upon to examine the safety of such conventional foods obtained from novel varieties of organisms, but this is not always the case.

In contrast, most national authorities consider that specific assessments are necessary for GM foods. Specific systems have been set up for the rigorous evaluation of GM organisms and GM foods relative to both human health and the environment. Similar evaluations are generally not performed for conventional foods. Hence there currently exists a significant difference in the evaluation process prior to marketing for these two groups of food.

The WHO Department of Food Safety and Zoonoses aims at assisting national authorities in the identification of foods that should be subject to risk assessment and to recommend appropriate approaches to safety assessment. Should national authorities decide to conduct safety assessment of GM organisms, WHO recommends the use of Codex Alimentarius guidelines (See the answer to Question 11 below).

4. How is a safety assessment of GM food conducted?

The safety assessment of GM foods generally focuses on: (a) direct health effects (toxicity); (b) potential to provoke allergic reaction (allergenicity); (c) specific components thought to have nutritional or toxic properties; (d) the stability of the inserted gene; (e) nutritional effects associated with genetic modification; and (f) any unintended effects which could result from the gene insertion.

5. What are the main issues of concern for human health?

While theoretical discussions have covered a broad range of aspects, the three main issues debated are the potentials to provoke allergic reaction (allergenicity), gene transfer and outcrossing.

Allergenicity

As a matter of principle, the transfer of genes from commonly allergenic organisms to non-allergic organisms is discouraged unless it can be demonstrated that the protein product of the transferred gene is not allergenic. While foods developed using traditional breeding methods are not generally tested for allergenicity, protocols for the testing of GM foods have been evaluated by the Food and Agriculture Organization of the United Nations (FAO) and WHO. No allergic effects have been found relative to GM foods currently on the market.

Gene transfer

Gene transfer from GM foods to cells of the body or to bacteria in the gastrointestinal tract would cause concern if the transferred genetic material adversely affects human health. This would be particularly relevant if antibiotic resistance genes, used as markers when creating GMOs, were to be transferred. Although the probability of transfer is low, the use of gene transfer technology that does not involve antibiotic resistance genes is encouraged.

Outcrossing

The migration of genes from GM plants into conventional crops or related species in the wild (referred to as "outcrossing"), as well as the mixing of crops derived from conventional seeds with GM crops, may have an indirect effect on food safety and food security. Cases have been reported where GM crops approved for animal feed or industrial use were detected at low levels in the products intended for human consumption. Several countries have adopted strategies to reduce mixing, including a clear separation of the fields within which GM crops and conventional crops are grown.

6. How is a risk assessment for the environment performed?

Environmental risk assessments cover both the GMO concerned and the potential receiving environment. The assessment process includes evaluation of the characteristics of the GMO and its effect and stability in the environment, combined with ecological characteristics of the environment in which the introduction will take place. The assessment also includes unintended effects which could result from the insertion of the new gene.

7. What are the issues of concern for the environment?

Issues of concern include: the capability of the GMO to escape and potentially introduce the engineered genes into wild populations; the persistence of the gene after the GMO has been harvested; the susceptibility of non-target organisms (e.g. insects which are not pests) to the gene product; the stability of the gene; the reduction in the spectrum of other plants including loss of biodiversity; and increased use of chemicals in agriculture. The environmental safety aspects of GM crops vary considerably according to local conditions.

8. Are GM foods safe?

Different GM organisms include different genes inserted in different ways. This means that individual GM foods and their safety should be assessed on a case-by-case basis and that it is not possible to make general statements on the safety of all GM foods.

GM foods currently available on the international market have passed safety assessments and are not likely to present risks for human health. In addition, no effects on human health have been shown as a result of the consumption of such foods by the general population in the countries where they have been approved. Continuous application of safety assessments based on the Codex Alimentarius principles and, where appropriate, adequate post market monitoring, should form the basis for ensuring the safety of GM foods.

9. How are GM foods regulated nationally?

The way governments have regulated GM foods varies. In some countries GM foods are not yet regulated. Countries which have legislation in place focus primarily on assessment of risks for consumer health. Countries which have regulatory provisions for GM foods usually also regulate GMOs in general, taking into account health and environmental risks, as well as control- and trade-related issues (such as potential testing and labelling regimes). In view of the dynamics of the debate on GM foods, legislation is likely to continue to evolve.

10. What kind of GM foods are on the market internationally?

GM crops available on the international market today have been designed using one of three basic traits: resistance to insect damage; resistance to viral infections; and tolerance towards certain herbicides. GM crops with higher nutrient content (e.g. soybeans increased oleic acid) have been also studied recently.

11. What happens when GM foods are traded internationally?

The Codex Alimentarius Commission (Codex) is the joint FAO/WHO intergovernmental body responsible for developing the standards, codes of practice, guidelines and recommendations that constitute the Codex Alimentarius, meaning the international food code. Codex developed principles for the human health risk analysis of GM foods in 2003.

- Principles for the risk analysis of foods derived from modern biotechnology
  The premise of these principles sets out a premarket assessment, performed on a case-by-case basis and including an evaluation of both direct effects (from the inserted gene) and unintended effects (that may arise as a consequence of insertion of the new gene) Codex also developed three Guidelines:
- Guideline for the conduct of food safety assessment of foods derived from recombinant-DNA plants
- Guideline for the conduct of food safety assessment of foods produced using recombinant-DNA microorganisms
- Guideline for the conduct of food safety assessment of foods derived from recombinant-DNA animals

Codex principles do not have a binding effect on national legislation, but are referred to specifically in the Agreement on the Application of Sanitary and Phytosanitary Measures of the World Trade Organization (SPS Agreement), and WTO Members are encouraged to harmonize national standards with Codex standards. If trading partners have the same or similar mechanisms for the safety assessment of GM foods, the possibility that one product is approved in one country but rejected in another becomes smaller.

The Cartagena Protocol on Biosafety, an environmental treaty legally binding for its Parties which took effect in 2003, regulates transboundary movements of Living Modified Organisms (LMOs). GM foods are within the scope of the Protocol only if they contain LMOs that are capable of transferring or replicating genetic material. The cornerstone of the Protocol is a requirement that exporters seek consent from importers before the first shipment of LMOs intended for release into the environment.

12. Have GM products on the international market passed a safety assessment?

The GM products that are currently on the international market have all passed safety assessments conducted by national authorities. These different assessments in general follow the same basic principles, including an assessment of environmental and human health risk. The food safety assessment is usually based on Codex documents.

13. Why has there been concern about GM foods among some politicians, public interest groups and consumers?

Since the first introduction on the market in the mid-1990s of a major GM food (herbicide-resistant soybeans), there has been concern about such food among politicians, activists and consumers, especially in Europe. Several factors are involved. In the late 1980s–early 1990s, the results of decades of molecular research reached the public domain. Until that time, consumers were generally not very aware of the potential of this research. In the case of food, consumers started to wonder about safety because they perceive that modern biotechnology is leading to the creation of new species.

Consumers frequently ask, "what is in it for me?" Where medicines are concerned, many consumers more readily accept biotechnology as beneficial for their health (e.g. vaccines, medicines with improved treatment potential or increased safety). In the case of the first GM foods introduced onto the European market, the products were of no apparent direct benefit to consumers (not significantly cheaper, no increased shelflife, no better taste). The potential for GM seeds to result in bigger yields per cultivated area should lead to lower prices. However, public attention has focused on the risk side of the risk-benefit equation, often without distinguishing between potential environmental impacts and public health effects of GMOs.

Consumer confidence in the safety of food supplies in Europe has decreased significantly as a result of a number of food scares that took place in the second half of the 1990s that are unrelated to GM foods. This has also had an impact on discussions about the acceptability of GM foods. Consumers have questioned the validity of risk assessments, both with regard to consumer health and environmental risks, focusing in particular on long-term effects. Other topics debated by consumer organizations have included allergenicity and antimicrobial resistance. Consumer concerns have triggered a discussion on the desirability of labelling GM foods, allowing for an informed choice of consumers.

14. What is the state of public debate on GMOs?

The release of GMOs into the environment and the marketing of GM foods have resulted in a public debate in many parts of the world. This debate is likely to continue, probably in the broader context of other uses of biotechnology (e.g. in human medicine) and their consequences for human societies. Even though the issues under debate are usually very similar (costs and benefits, safety issues), the outcome of the debate differs from country to country. On issues such as labelling and traceability of GM foods as a way to address consumer preferences, there is no worldwide consensus to date. Despite the lack of consensus on these topics, the Codex Alimentarius Commission has made significant progress and developed Codex texts relevant to labelling of foods derived from modern biotechnology in 2011 to ensure consistency on any approach on labelling implemented by Codex members with already adopted Codex provisions.

15. Are people's reactions related to the different attitudes to food in various regions of the world?

Depending on the region of the world, people often have different attitudes to food. In addition to nutritional value, food often has societal and historical connotations, and in some instances may have religious importance. Technological modification of food and food production may evoke a negative response among consumers, especially in the absence of sound risk communication on risk assessment efforts and cost/benefit evaluations.

16. Are there implications for the rights of farmers to own their crops?

Yes, intellectual property rights are likely to be an element in the debate on GM foods, with an impact on the rights of farmers. In the FAO/WHO expert consultation in 2003 (http://www.who.int/entity/foodsafety/biotech/meetings/en/gmanimal_reportnov03_en.pdf), WHO and FAO have considered potential problems of the technological divide and the unbalanced distribution of benefits and risks between developed and developing countries and the problem often becomes even more acute through the existence of intellectual property rights and patenting that places an advantage on the strongholds of scientific and technological expertise. Such considerations are likely to also affect the debate on GM foods.

17. Why are certain groups concerned about the growing influence of the chemical industry on agriculture?

Certain groups are concerned about what they consider to be an undesirable level of control of seed markets by a few chemical companies. Sustainable agriculture and biodiversity benefit most from the use of a rich variety of crops, both in terms of good crop protection practices as well as from the perspective of society at large and the values attached to food. These groups fear that as a result of the interest of the chemical industry in seed markets, the range of varieties used by farmers may be reduced mainly to GM crops. This would impact on the food basket of a society as well as in the long run on crop protection (for example, with the development of resistance against insect pests and tolerance of certain herbicides). The exclusive use of herbicide-tolerant GM crops would also make the farmer dependent on these chemicals. These groups fear a dominant position of the chemical industry in agricultural development, a trend which they do not consider to be sustainable.

18. What further developments can be expected in the area of GMOs?

Future GM organisms are likely to include plants with improved resistance against plant disease or drought, crops with increased nutrient levels, fish species with enhanced growth characteristics. For non-food use, they may include plants or animals producing pharmaceutically important proteins such as new vaccines.

19. What has WHO been doing to improve the evaluation of GM foods?

WHO has been taking an active role in relation to GM foods, primarily for two reasons:

- on the grounds that public health could benefit from the potential of biotechnology, for example, from an increase in the nutrient content of foods, decreased allergenicity and more efficient and/or sustainable food production; and
- based on the need to examine the potential negative effects on human health of the consumption of food produced through genetic modification in order to protect public health. Modern technologies should be thoroughly evaluated if they are to constitute a true improvement in the way food is produced.

WHO, together with FAO, has convened several expert consultations on the evaluation of GM foods and provided technical advice for the Codex Alimentarius Commission which was fed into the Codex Guidelines on safety assessment of GM foods. WHO will keep paying due attention to the safety of GM foods from the view of public health protection, in close collaboration with FAO and other international bodies.

Genetically Modifying Plants Can Save Endangered Species

Muhammad Nakhooda

Muhammad Nakhooda is a senior lecturer in biotechnology at Cape Peninsula University of Technology in South Africa.

As the human population swells—and in the face of a changing and unpredictable climate—the demand for natural resources increases. This leads to distressing rates of deforestation to prepare land for agriculture, medicinal and forestry products. Related to this is an alarming reduction in species worldwide.

This can only be ameliorated through urgent, intensive and sustainable agroforestry and conservation initiatives. This involves the conservation of natural forests as well as renewable plantation efforts. But to date only a scattering of such projects are in place worldwide.

Conservation and renewable plantation efforts are trailing behind the rate of resource exploitation and species disappearance. The problem is worsened by the vast number of endangered plant species. Once disturbed from their natural habitat, they can't easily be reintroduced. This is because many of them do not readily produce seeds, or their seeds cannot be stored to ensure longevity of the species. The result is a decreasing gene pool.

This poses further risks, as vulnerable species become marginalised. They are only suitable to shrinking ranges and more susceptible to disease. To intensify conservation while enhancing agroforestry, smarter plant breeding practices are required.

Traditional breeding has allowed for the identification, selection and propagation of plants with a superior genetic makeup, or genotype, from a given plant population. But traditional methods often fail to isolate the required superior characteristics of a species. They can also take more than five or six breeding cycles before a valuable trait is established and maintained in a plant population. The process can take decades for perennial plants, like trees.

Plant biotechnology is increasingly being used to complement traditional screening and breeding practices. Plants can be grown in test tubes under controlled laboratory conditions. Advances in biochemistry and genetics have also ushered in an understanding of the factors that influence plant growth.

Together these developments have created the opportunity to precisely identify and mass propagate superior plant varieties within a fraction of the time of traditional methods. On top of this, if required, the precise altering of the genetic makeup of plants is now also possible. This enables plant genomes to be radically enhanced so that superior genotypes can be created, maintained and propagated.

Preserving valuable genes

Maintaining superior genetics for valuable traits is fundamental in agroforestry. But to maintain superior genetics, seed production is rarely an option. In producing a seed, the sexual cross between genetically different male and female parent plants results in the dilution of valuable genes. This often leads to offspring with unpredictable genetics.

For the agroforestry industry to succeed, genotypes with predictably fast growth rates, high yields, and disease and drought resistance are needed. This will ensure land-use efficiency is maximised, which in turn will decrease ecological disturbance and protect indigenous plant species and sensitive natural forests.

One method that holds promise for preserving valuable genes is somatic embryogenesis. This is the ability to produce viable embryos from virtually any plant organ, while avoiding sexual

2013. HT cotton occupied 82 percent of cotton acreage and HT corn 85 percent of corn acreage in 2013. Insect infestations tend to be more localized than weed infestations. Farmers planted Bt cotton (engineered to control insects such as tobacco budworm, bollworm, and pink bollworm) on 75 percent of cotton acreage in 2013. Bt corn—which controls the European corn borer, the corn rootworm, and the corn earworm—was planted on 76 percent of corn acres in 2013.

While corn, cotton, and soybeans account for the vast majority of GE acreage in the U.S., other GE crops commercially grown include HT canola, HT sugar beets, HT alfalfa, virus-resistant papaya, and virus-resistant squash. Since being commercially introduced, the varieties of GE seeds commercially available with pest management traits have increased in complexity, incorporating resistance to a broader range of insects and tolerance to more herbicides, as well as combining (or "stacking") both HT and Bt traits. With these innovations, the price of GE seeds increased, both in nominal and real terms. The rapid adoption of GE varieties by farmers is consistent with the belief that GE seeds provide improved performance or other benefits that make their use worthwhile, but what do research findings suggest?

GE seeds and yield losses to pests

In the absence of pests, commercially available GE seeds do not increase maximum crop yields. However, by protecting a plant from certain pests, GE crops can prevent yield losses to pests, allowing the plant to approach its yield potential. Bt crops are particularly effective at mitigating yield losses.

Average Bt corn yields have increased as new insect resistance traits have been incorporated into the seeds and seeds with multiple (stacked) traits have become available. In 1996, Bt corn was only resistant to one type of pest: the European corn borer. Since then, Bt corn resistance to corn rootworms (2003) and corn earworms (2010) has been introduced. Most experimental field tests and farm surveys show that Bt crops produce higher average yields than conventional crops. Data from USDA's Agricultural Resource Management Survey (ARMS) show that Bt corn yields were 17 bushels per acre higher than conventional corn yields in 2005 and about 26 bushels higher in 2010. Moreover, using an econometric model that controls for other factors, ERS researchers found that a 10-percent increase in the rate of Bt corn adoption was associated with a 1.7-percent increase in yields in 2005 and a 2.3-percent increase in yields in 2010. Researchers also found that a 10-percent increase in the adoption of Bt cotton in 1997 was associated with a 2.1-percent increase in yields.

On the other hand, evidence on the impact of HT seeds on soybean, corn, and cotton yields is mixed. Some researchers found no significant difference between the yields of adopters and non-adopters of HT; others found that HT adopters had higher yields, while still others found that adopters had lower yields.

An analysis of ARMS corn data indicates that stacked seeds (seeds with several GE traits) have higher yields than conventional seeds or seeds with only one GE trait. For example, 2010 ARMS data show that conventional corn seeds had an average yield of 134 bushels per acre. By contrast, seeds with two types of herbicide tolerance (glyphosate and glufosinate) and three types of insect resistance (corn borer, corn rootworm, and corn earworm) had an average yield of 171 bushels per acre.

Not surprisingly, adoption rates of stacked-seed varieties have increased quickly. Use of stacked corn seed grew from 1 percent of planted acres in 2000 to 71 percent in 2013. GE varieties incorporating three or four traits are now common.

Bt seeds, net returns, and household income

The market price of seed incorporates the costs associated with seed development, production, marketing, and distribution. The price of GE soybean and corn seeds grew by about 50 percent in real terms (adjusted for inflation) between 2001 and 2010. The price of GE cotton seed grew even faster. The increase in GE seed prices can be attributed in part to increasing price premiums over conventional seeds associated with the rising share of GE seeds with multiple (stacked) traits and /or more than one mode of action for particular target pests Another factor contributing to the increase in seed prices is the improvement in seed genetics (germplasm).

The profitability of GE seeds for individual farmers depends largely on the value of the yield losses mitigated and the pesticide and seed costs, which vary by crop and technology. Most studies show that adoption of Bt cotton and Bt corn is associated with increased net returns/variable profits. However, some studies of Bt corn show that profitability is strongly dependent on pest infestation levels (adoption of Bt cotton and Bt corn was associated with increased returns when the pest pressure was high).

The evidence on the impact of HT seeds on net returns is less consistent. Several researchers found that the adoption of herbicide-tolerant cotton had a positive impact on net returns. However, other researchers found no significant difference between the net returns of adopters and non-adopters of HT soybeans, and others found that HT soybean farmers are less profitable than their conventional counterparts. Overall, the empirical evidence on the impact of adopting herbicide-tolerant soybeans on net returns is inconclusive.

The fact that adoption of HT crops has been continuously rising, even though several researchers found no significant differences between the net returns of adopters and non-adopters, suggests that adopters derive other benefits. In particular, weed control for HT soybeans may be simpler and more flexible (e.g., HT seed-based production programs allow growers to use one product to control a wide range of both broadleaf and grass weeds instead of using several herbicides to achieve adequate weed control), freeing up valuable management time for leisure, or to generate enterprise growth or off-farm income.

ERS research shows that HT adoption is associated with increased off-farm household income for U.S. soybean farmers, most likely because time savings associated with HT crops were used in off-farm employment. More recently, other researchers confirmed that GE crops led to household labor savings and that farmers adopting GE crops derived value from the convenience, flexibility, and increased worker safety associated with growing HT crops that enable them to use fewer toxic herbicides.

Adoption and pesticide use

Studies based on field tests and farm surveys have examined the extent to which GE crop adoption affects pesticide (insecticide and herbicide) use, and most results show a reduction in pesticide use. A 2010 National Research Council study concurred that GE crops lead to reduced pesticide use and /or to use of pesticides with lower toxicity compared to those used on conventional crops.

Generally, Bt adoption is associated with lower levels of insecticide use. Pounds of insecticide (per planted acre) applied to corn and cotton crops have decreased steadily over the last 10 years (except for cotton in 1999-2001, when application levels were distorted during the boll weevil eradication program).

Insecticide use trends suggest that insect infestation levels on corn and cotton farms were lower in 2010 than in earlier years and are consistent with the fact that European corn borer populations have steadily declined over the last decade. In addition, several researchers have shown that areawide suppression of certain insects such as the European corn borer and the pink bollworm are associated with Bt corn and Bt cotton use, respectively. This suggests that Bt seeds have benefited not only adopters but non-adopters as well.

Herbicide use on corn, cotton and soybean acres (measured in pounds per planted acre) declined slightly in the first years following introduction of HT seeds in 1996, but increased modestly in later years. Despite the relatively minor effect HT crop adoption has had on overall herbicide usage, HT crop adoption has enabled farmers to substitute glyphosate (which many HT crops are designed to tolerate) for more traditional herbicides. Because glyphosate is significantly less toxic and less persistent than traditional herbicides, the net impact of HT crop adoption is an improvement in environmental quality and a reduction in health risks.

HT crops and conservation tillage

Conservation tillage (including no-till, ridge-till, and mulch-till) is known to provide environmental benefits and is facilitated by use of HT crops. By leaving at least 30 percent of crop residue covering the soil surface after all the tillage and planting operations, conservation tillage reduces soil erosion by wind and water, increases water retention, and reduces soil degradation and water/ chemical runoff. In addition, conservation tillage reduces the carbon footprint of agriculture.

By 2006, approximately 86 percent of HT soybean planted acres were under conservation tillage, compared to only 36 percent of conventional soybean acres. Differences in the use of no-till were just as pronounced. While approximately 45 percent of HT soybean acres were cultivated using no-till technologies in 2006, only 5 percent of the acres planted with conventional seeds were cultivated using no-till techniques, which are often considered the most effective of all conservation tillage systems. Cotton and corn data exhibit similar though less pronounced patterns.

These trends suggest that HT crop adoption facilitates the use of conservation tillage practices. In addition, a review of several econometric studies points to a two-way causal relationship between the adoption of HT crops and conservation tillage. Thus, in addition to its direct effects on herbicide usage, adoption of herbicide-tolerant crops indirectly benefits the environment by encouraging the use of conservation tillage.

Future trends

The acceptance of GE crops by farmers has been due, in large part, to the pest management traits incorporated into GE seeds. Farmers were willing to adopt GE seeds because their benefits exceeded their costs, while domestic consumers were largely indifferent to these traits. But how long can farmers expect to benefit from the pest management traits engineered into the seeds currently commercially available? And, what other traits might be engineered into seeds that would attract farmer and consumer interest?

As with other efforts to control agricultural pests, pests will inevitably develop resistance to the pest management traits incorporated in GE seeds. Prior to the commercial introduction of Bt crops, entomologists and other scientists persuasively argued that mandatory minimum refuge requirements (planting sufficient acres of the non-Bt crop near the Bt crop) were needed to reduce the rate at which targeted insect pests evolved resistance. Analysis of more than a decade of monitoring data suggests that minimum refuge requirements and natural refuges have indeed helped delay the evolution of Bt resistance in some insect pests. However, Bt resistance in western corn rootworm, cotton bollworm, and fall armyworm populations leading to reduced efficacy of Bt corn and Bt cotton has been recently documented in some U.S. crop fields.

Likewise, an overreliance on glyphosate and a reduction in the diversity of weed management practices by HT crop producers contributed to the evolution of glyphosate resistance in 14 weed species in the United States. Because no new major classes of herbicides have been made commercially available in the last 20 years, and because few new ones are expected to be available soon, growing resistance to glyphosate is expected to reduce the benefit farmers derive from using the most widely available HT seed varieties. Furthermore, the weed management practices needed to slow the spread of glyphosate-resistant weeds may themselves reduce the short-term benefits of planting glyphosate-tolerant (i.e., HT) seeds. As a result, their benefits may erode over time in the absence of further developments affecting HT seeds and their associated herbicides and/or improvements in weed management practices. One such development is the introduction of crops tolerant to the herbicides dicamba and 2, 4-D if used in the context of a diversified approach to weed management.

While relatively few GE traits are currently commercially available, the number of field releases to test GE varieties approved by USDA's Animal and Plant Health Inspection Service indicates continued GE-related R&D activities since field testing is a critical part of seed development. The number of field releases grew from 4 in 1985 to 1,194 in 2002 and has since averaged around 800 per year. Other measures suggest that GE-related R&D activity has increased dramatically since 2005.

Field releases approved for GE varieties continue to focus heavily on herbicide tolerance and insect resistance, but other traits are being developed and tested in large numbers as well. These include traits that provide favorable agronomic properties (resistance to cold/drought/frost/salinity, more efficient use of nitrogen, increased yield); enhanced product quality, such as delayed ripening, flavor and texture (fruits and vegetables); increased protein or carbohydrate content, fatty acid content, or micronutrient content; modified starch, color (cotton, flowers), fiber properties (cotton), or gluten content (wheat); naturally decaffeinated (coffee); and nutraceuticals (added vitamins, iron, antioxidants such as beta-carotene).

New HT and insect resistance traits may give farmers more pest management options and slow the spread of pesticide resistance among pest populations. Approval of other "first generation" traits that improve yields or reduce yield losses could result in further adoption of GE varieties. Farmer response to the approval of "second generation" traits that alter end product quality may be more cautious. Farmers can expect to benefit from the adoption of these GE traits only if consumer acceptance is assured. In short, the future of GE seed use depends on the ability of farmers to adopt best management practices, the ability of biotech companies to develop new GE varieties, and consumer acceptance of products from GE sources.

GMO Foods Are Unsafe, Unhealthy, and Harm the Environment

Jeffrey Smith

Jeffrey Smith is the founder of the website Institute for Responsible Technology, which seeks to educate consumers about genetically modified foods and crops.

1. Gmos are unhealthy.

The American Academy of Environmental Medicine (AAEM) urges doctors to prescribe non-GMO diets for all patients. They cite animal studies showing organ damage, gastrointestinal and immune system disorders, accelerated aging, and infertility. Human studies show how genetically modified (GM) food can leave material behind inside us, possibly causing long-term problems. Genes inserted into GM soy, for example, can transfer into the DNA of bacteria living inside us, and that the toxic insecticide produced by GM corn was found in the blood of pregnant women and their unborn fetuses.

Numerous health problems increased after GMOs were introduced in 1996. The percentage of Americans with three or more chronic illnesses jumped from 7% to 13% in just 9 years; food allergies skyrocketed, and disorders such as autism, reproductive disorders, digestive problems, and others are on the rise. Although there is not sufficient research to confirm that GMOs are a contributing factor, doctors groups such as the AAEM tell us not to wait before we start protecting ourselves, and especially our children who are most at risk.

The American Public Health Association and American Nurses Association are among many medical groups that condemn the use of GM bovine growth hormone, because the milk from treated cows has more of the hormone IGF-1 (insulin-like growth factor 1)—which is linked to cancer.

"10 Reasons to Avoid GMOs," Jeffrey Smith, Institute for Responsible Technology, August 25, 2011. Reprinted by permission.

2. GMOs contaminate forever.

GMOs cross pollinate and their seeds can travel. It is impossible to fully clean up our contaminated gene pool. Self-propagating GMO pollution will outlast the effects of global warming and nuclear waste. The potential impact is huge, threatening the health of future generations. GMO contamination has also caused economic losses for organic and non-GMO farmers who often struggle to keep their crops pure.

3. GMOs increase herbicide use.

Most GM crops are engineered to be "herbicide tolerant"— they [resist] deadly weed killer. Monsanto, for example, sells Roundup Ready crops, designed to survive applications of their Roundup herbicide.

Between 1996 and 2008, US farmers sprayed an extra 383 million pounds of herbicide on GMOs. Overuse of Roundup results in "superweeds," resistant to the herbicide. This is causing farmers to use even more toxic herbicides every year. Not only does this create environmental harm, GM foods contain higher residues of toxic herbicides. Roundup, for example, is linked with sterility, hormone disruption, birth defects, and cancer.

4. Genetic engineering creates dangerous side effects.

By mixing genes from totally unrelated species, genetic engineering unleashes a host of unpredictable side effects. Moreover, irrespective of the type of genes that are inserted, the very process of creating a GM plant can result in massive collateral damage that produces new toxins, allergens, carcinogens, and nutritional deficiencies.

5. Government oversight is dangerously lax.

Most of the health and environmental risks of GMOs are ignored by governments' superficial regulations and safety assessments. The reason for this tragedy is largely political. The US Food and Drug

Administration (FDA), for example, doesn't require a single safety study, does not mandate labeling of GMOs, and allows companies to put their GM foods onto the market without even notifying the agency. Their justification was the claim that they had no information showing that GM foods were substantially different. But this was a lie. Secret agency memos made public by a lawsuit show that the overwhelming consensus even among the FDA's own scientists was that GMOs can create unpredictable, hard-to-detect side effects. They urged long-term safety studies. But the White House had instructed the FDA to promote biotechnology, and the agency official in charge of policy was Michael Taylor, Monsanto's former attorney, later their vice president. He's now the US Food Safety Czar.

6. The biotech industry uses "tobacco science" to claim product safety.

Biotech companies like Monsanto told us that Agent Orange, PCBs, and DDT were safe. They are now using the same type of superficial, rigged research to try and convince us that GMOs are safe. Independent scientists, however, have caught the spin-masters red-handed, demonstrating without doubt how industry-funded research is designed to avoid finding problems, and how adverse findings are distorted or denied.

7. Independent research and reporting is attacked and suppressed.

Scientists who discover problems with GMOs have been attacked, gagged, fired, threatened, and denied funding. The journal Nature acknowledged that a "large block of scientists . . . denigrate research by other legitimate scientists in a knee-jerk, partisan, emotional way that is not helpful in advancing knowledge." Attempts by media to expose problems are also often censored.

8. GMOs harm the environment.

GM crops and their associated herbicides can harm birds, insects, amphibians, marine ecosystems, and soil organisms. They reduce bio-diversity, pollute water resources, and are unsustainable. For example, GM crops are eliminating habitat for monarch butterflies, whose populations are down 50% in the US. Roundup herbicide has been shown to cause birth defects in amphibians, embryonic deaths and endocrine disruptions, and organ damage in animals even at very low doses. GM canola has been found growing wild in North Dakota and California, threatening to pass on its herbicide tolerant genes on to weeds.

9. GMOs do not increase yields, and work against feeding a hungry world.

Whereas sustainable non-GMO agricultural methods used in developing countries have conclusively resulted in yield increases of 79% and higher, GMOs do not, on average, increase yields at all. This was evident in the Union of Concerned Scientists' 2009 report Failure to Yield—the definitive study to date on GM crops and yield.

The International Assessment of Agricultural Knowledge, Science and Technology for Development (IAASTD) report, authored by more than 400 scientists and backed by 58 governments, stated that GM crop yields were "highly variable" and in some cases, "yields declined." The report noted, "Assessment of the technology lags behind its development, information is anecdotal and contradictory, and uncertainty about possible benefits and damage is unavoidable." They determined that the current GMOs have nothing to offer the goals of reducing hunger and poverty, improving nutrition, health and rural livelihoods, and facilitating social and environmental sustainability.

On the contrary, GMOs divert money and resources that would otherwise be spent on more safe, reliable, and appropriate technologies.

10. By avoiding GMOs, you contribute to the coming tipping point of consumer rejection, forcing them out of our food supply.

Because GMOs give no consumer benefits, if even a small percentage of us start rejecting brands that contain them, GM ingredients will become a marketing liability. Food companies will kick them out. In Europe, for example, the tipping point was achieved in 1999, just after a high profile GMO safety scandal hit the papers and alerted citizens to the potential dangers. In the US, a consumer rebellion against GM bovine growth hormone has also reached a tipping point, kicked the cow drug out of dairy products by Wal-Mart, Starbucks, Dannon, Yoplait, and most of America's dairies.

Genetically Modified Foods Pose Ethical Questions

Christopher Mayes

Christopher Mayes is a postdoctoral research fellow at the Centre for Values, Ethics and the Law in Medicine at the University of Sydney. His latest book is The Biopolitics of Lifestyle: Foucault, Ethics and Health Choices.

Food is cultural, social and deeply personal, so it's no surprise that modifications to the way food is produced, distributed and consumed often lead to ethical debates.

Developments in the genetic modification (GM) of foods and crops has resulted in a raft of controversies.

Ethics can help here. While science determines whether we can safely modify the genetic makeup of certain organisms, ethics asks whether we should.

Ethics tries to move beyond factual statements about what is, to evaluative statements about the way we *should* act towards ourselves, each other and the environment we inhabit. But things are not always so clear-cut.

Three areas of ethics can help frame some of the concerns with GM food and crops: virtue, moral status and consequences.

Virtues vs vices

Ethics of GM foods can be developed by looking at virtue or character. Does the activity of engaging in the development of GM foods and crops erode virtues while producing vices? Or is GM technology a prudent use of knowledge for humanitarian goals?

Character or virtue-based arguments are seen in the case of golden rice—a rice strain modified to contain beta-carotene, a precursor of vitamin A.

According to the World Health Organisation more than 250 million preschool age children are vitamin A deficient (VAD), and two million deaths and more than half a million cases of blindness are attributed to VAD. The developers of golden rice say it will supply 60% of the recommended daily intake of vitamin A.

But global outrage ensued after group of Filipino farmers destroyed a test crop of golden rice. There has been little recognition of the Sisyphean struggle of farmers in countries such as the Philippines, Bangladesh and India, yet these farmers have been described as anti-science Luddites and contributing to the deaths of children.

Critics of golden rice such as Wendell Berry and Vandana Shiva argue that GM technology is a solution offered by industrial agriculture to address problems created by industrial agriculture.

Golden rice is a techno-scientific fix to structural problems created by some of the very companies that may profit from GM crops.

Although golden rice is a non-profit initiative, Shiva argues that it is a trojan horse to give GM crops a humanitarian face.

According to opponents such as Shiva, golden rice and GM crops not only pose negative consequences for farmers, environment and the global poor, but represent vices of greed, arrogance and dominance. Rather than humbly working with and caring for the natural environment, industrial and technological interventions seek to master, profit and control.

Morality of nature

There are also concerns about the moral status of the organism itself—does the modification of an organism's genetic makeup represent a wrong to the dignity or integrity to the organism?

This position depends on arguments that nature has dignity and interests beyond those of its human inhabitants. Such arguments are not readily accepted due to their metaphysical or theological overtones and dependence on essentialist idea of nature.

Appeals to nature can led to what British philosopher G.E. Moore described as the naturalistic fallacy—the idea that we can derive moral statements from facts of nature. Examples include:

- raw milk is good because it's natural
- standing desks are good because we weren't meant to sit
- genetically modified crops are wrong because they're unnatural.

Perhaps we aren't so concerned about the essential dignity of rice or wheat, but what about GM pigs that glow in the dark, featherless chickens, cows that produce human milk or the integrity of an ecosystem? Although the arguments are relatively the same, in discussing GM animals, the idea of a natural integrity or dignity seems more compelling.

Weighing up consequences

The most common way of framing the ethics of GM foods is to ask: do GM foods and crops present negative or harmful consequences for individuals, populations or the environment? Answers to this question vary according to context.

Most scientists argue that GM foods are safe to eat and will not harm consumer health.

While critics maintain that long-term health effects are uncertain, they contend that even if GM foods are safe to eat other harmful consequences should be considered, such as the impact of patenting lawson farmers and research integrity, or the risk of GM crops contaminatingother crops or escaping into the wild.

Debates over consequences tend to avoid the question of whether there is something inherently objectionable about GM foods and crops. So long as there is appropriate management of risks, then theoretically, there is no ethical problem.

It is unlikely these issues will be resolved any time soon—and likely that new ones will be added—but one area that can be worked on is discourse ethics.

Describing opponents of golden rice, even those that destroy test crops, as committing crimes against humanity or those in favour as pursing economic self-interest does little to move the debate forward.

Until productive discourse is established, barriers between opposing views will only strengthen.

Is the Genetic Engineering of Animals Ethical?

Overview: Animals Are Genetically Engineered for a Variety of Purposes and Are Closely Regulated

US Food and Drug Administration

The US Food and Drug Administration is the federal agency that protects public health by assuring that foods are safe, wholesome, sanitary, and properly labeled.

Q: What is genetic engineering?

A: Genetic engineering generally refers to the use of tools of modern biotechnology and molecular biology to introduce new genetic material, or delete or alter existing genetic material to introduce intended, new traits or characteristics.

Q: What is a genetically engineered animal?

A: A genetically engineered (GE) animal is one that contains additional or altered genetic material (e.g., recombinant DNA (rDNA)) through use of modern biotechnology tools that's intended to give the animal a new trait or characteristic. Examples of the kind of GE animals that are being developed are provided below.

Q: What kinds of GE animals are being developed?

A: Many kinds of GE animals are in development.

- *Biopharm* animals are those that have undergone genetic engineering to produce particular substances, such as human insulin, for pharmaceutical use.
- *Research* animals may be engineered to make them more susceptible to particular diseases, such as cancer, in order to gain a better basic understanding of the disease for the development of new therapies or in order to evaluate new medical therapies.

"Consumer Q & A," US Food and Drug Administration.

- *Xenotransplant* animals are being engineered so they can be used as sources for cells, tissues or organs that can be used for transplantation into humans.
- *Companion* animals that are modified to enrich or enhance their interaction with humans (i.e., hypoallergenic pets).
- *Disease resistant* animals may be used either for food use or biopharm applications. These animals have received modifications that make them resistant to common diseases, such as mastitis (a very painful infection of the udder) in dairy cows, or particularly deadly diseases, such as bovine spongiform encephalopathy (BSE).
- *Food use* animals have been engineered to provide healthier meat, such as pigs that contain healthy omega-3 fatty acids at levels comparable to those in fish.

Q: How are GE animals regulated?

A: FDA regulates GE animals under the "new animal drug" [The new animal drug approval requirements are described in the Code of Federal Regulations under 21 CFR 514.] provisions of the Federal Food, Drug, and Cosmetic Act (FD&C Act) and FDA's implementing regulations for new animal drugs. This guidance is intended to help industry understand the requirements that are established by statute and regulations as they apply to these animals, including those of the National Environmental Policy Act (NEPA), and to inform the public about the process FDA is using to regulate GE animals. The guidance does not create any new obligations. It clarifies how the regulations apply to GE animals.

Q: What's the difference between animal clones and GE animals?

A: The animal clones that were the subject of FDA's risk assessment on animal cloning (released in January of 2008) are "just clones"— that is, they are copies of individual conventionally-bred animals, and do not contain any rDNA constructs. What can be confusing is that an animal clone can be genetically engineered (i.e., have an rDNA construct introduced into it), and a GE animal can be reproduced by cloning. Our guidance covers GE animals, irrespective of whether they were reproduced by cloning. It does not cover animal clones that do not contain an rDNA construct ("just clones").

Q: Why is FDA regulating GE animals differently from animal clones?
A: Clones are really just genetic copies of the animals from which they are produced. The purpose of the FDA risk assessment was to determine whether cloning posed any new risks to the health of animals and whether animal clones posed new food safety risks. The conclusion of that risk assessment was that there are no new risks associated with those animals, that food from cattle, swine, and goat clones, and the progeny of the clone of any species traditionally consumed as food was as safe to eat as that from conventionally bred animals, and that no new regulatory requirements are necessary beyond those that apply to other, conventionally-bred animals. By contrast, GE animals have changes to their genetic material that may potentially affect the health of the GE animal or the safety of food from the GE animal. Therefore, there are risk-based reasons for FDA to require their approval.

Q: Will GE animals be regulated the same if they're used for food or if they're intended to produce pharmaceuticals for people?
A: GE animals are subject to premarket oversight whether they are intended to be used for food or to produce pharmaceuticals or other useful products. There may be some differences in what the actual oversight process entails depending on the kinds of risk(s) the GE animals may pose, and the kinds of uses for which they are intended. In addition, the pharmaceuticals produced from GE animals must be approved through the same process as applies to other pharmaceuticals. In general, we do not anticipate that biopharm animals will be used for food.

Q: What kind of post-market surveillance will there be?
A: Post-market surveillance will vary depending on the GE animal. However, as with conventional new animal drugs, the guidance tells sponsors (individuals or companies submitting GE animal applications to FDA for review) that in their application they should demonstrate that the rDNA construct is stable in the animal over time, and that the GE animal retains the new characteristics over time. As with conventional drugs, if additional information shows that there are safety concerns, or if the GE animal no longer has the characteristics claimed for it, FDA can take steps to have the GE animal removed from the market.

Q: Will FDA be looking at effects on the health of animals?
A: Before FDA can approve a new animal drug, it must determine that the drug is safe for the animal receiving it. Therefore, before we can approve a GE animal, we must determine that the rDNA construct is safe for the animal containing it. To do that, we look at the health of the animal. In the guidance, we provide recommendations on how developers can assess the health of their animals.

Q: Is food from GE animals in the food supply?
A: On November 19, 2015, FDA approved an application related to AquAdvantage Salmon, a GE Atlantic salmon. Although these salmon will be bred in Canada, and raised in Panama, food from these salmon will be imported into the U.S. For details on the kinds of studies that were conducted to assess food safety, please see the Freedom of Information Summary, Section IX.

We will not approve any GE animal for food use unless we find that the food from those GE animals is safe. It would be illegal to introduce food from an unapproved GE animal into the food supply without FDA permission. We work closely with GE animal producers to make sure that they keep good records of their animals and that none enter the food supply without FDA approval.

Q: Will food from GE animals be labeled?

A: The FDA recognizes that many consumers are interested in whether food ingredients are derived from genetically engineered plants or animals, and is also publishing guidance for manufacturers who wish to voluntarily label their foods as containing or not containing such ingredients. If food from a GE animal is materially different from its non-engineered counterpart (for example, if it has a different nutritional profile), the difference would be material information that would have to be indicated in the labeling. Marketers may voluntarily label their foods as coming from GE or non-GE animals, as long as the labeling is truthful and not misleading. FDA oversees labeling of most fish and seafood, of milk and other dairy products, and of whole eggs in their shells. The U. S. Department of Agriculture's Food Safety and Inspection Service (FSIS) generally oversees labels used for meat, poultry, and other egg products.

Q: Will GE animals be labeled?

A: Developers of GE animals will need to have labeling accompanying the animals. The guidance recommends that the labeling describe the GE animal (e.g., common name/breed/line, genus, species, GE animal line, rDNA construct), and its intended use. Where the labeling for a GE animal contains animal care or safety information (e.g., husbandry or containment), we recommend that the labeling accompany the animal throughout all stages of its lifecycle.

Q: What other agencies are involved in the regulation of these animals?

A: Depending on the species and use of the animal in question, the U.S. Department of Agriculture's Animal and Plant Health Inspection Service (APHIS), FSIS, the Environmental Protection Agency, and others may play a role in the regulation of GE animals. FDA is working very closely with these agencies and Departments to coordinate the regulation of these animals.

Q: What about environmental effects?
A: Environmental evaluation that meets the requirements of NEPA is required prior to any approval. We expect that the environmental risks that may be posed by GE animals will differ on a case-by-case basis. For example, the concerns raised by a GE cow that is resistant to mastitis will be very different from the concerns raised by a GE fresh-water fish that is engineered to grow more rapidly. We will work closely with individual GE animal producers to make sure that their environmental assessments address all of the potential risks these animals may pose.

Q: Can food from biopharm animals be eaten?
A: In general, biopharm animals are not intended to be eaten: they are engineered to produce a therapeutic substance, and their value is in that product and not the meat or milk from the animal. Given the relatively small numbers of any particular line of biopharm animal, the large amount of food safety data that is required to be provided to FDA for each GE animal line intended to enter the food supply, and the kind of food safety issues that pharmaceutical chemicals present in such animals would generally pose, it would be very unusual for developers of biopharm animals to want to enter their animals into the food supply. Without FDA approval for food use, it would be illegal for a company to direct any of its GE animals into the food supply. It is much more likely that these animals will be disposed of in a way that does not involve human food use when they have reached the end of their lives.

However, if a developer provided sufficient evidence of safety and FDA approved the biopharm animal for food use, then the decision on whether to enter it into the food supply would be a marketing issue for the food producer and the developer and not a food safety issue.

Q: What are the potential benefits of GE animals for consumers?
A: Many GE animals in development are intended to have direct benefits to consumers. For instance, biopharm animals are being developed to produce various pharmaceuticals for humans or other

animals such as clotting factors, growth factors and inhibitors used in cancer therapy, some of which cannot now be produced in sufficient quantities to meet medical needs. Some GE animals are under development to produce healthier food. And other animals are under development to have indirect benefits to consumers, such as decreased environmental impact by excreting lower levels of pollutants in their wastes.

Q: Are there any GE animals on the market now?
A: In 2003, FDA chose to exercise enforcement discretion for a GE aquarium fish that fluoresces in the dark. FDA made this decision in part because the fish (Zebra danio) is not a species used for food, and in part because the agency was able to determine that it did not pose any additional environmental risks compared with conventional Zebra danios. (Zebra danios are unable to survive outside the very warm waters of the tropics, which effectively limits the ability of an escaped or released fish to affect the U.S. environment.)

Additionally, there are many different kinds of GE rats and mice used in laboratory research throughout the world.

In addition, as described below, FDA has approved three GE animal-related applications. The first was in 2009, when FDA's Center for Veterinary Medicine approved a GE goat that produced a human biologic in its milk. The Center for Biologics Evaluation and Research approved the human biologic, ATryn. In November 2015, FDA approved an application related to AquAdvantage Salmon, a GE Atlantic salmon. In December 2015, FDA's Center for Veterinary Medicine approved a GE chicken that produces a human biologic in its eggs. The Center for Drug Evaluation and Research approved the human biologic, Kanuma (sebelipase alfa).

Q: How long have GE animals existed? Why did FDA step in when it did?
A: The first GE animal, a rabbit, was produced in the 1980s. Since that time, the field has grown enormously. FDA has been monitoring and evaluating the development of GE animals and

believes that it is important now to provide the growing industry with a clear and transparent regulatory path. We also think it's important to let other stakeholders, including the public, know our policies and requirements on this issue. Because we are a science-based public health agency, we are using a rigorous regulatory approach to ensure the public health, while providing GE animal developers a path by which they can bring innovative products to the market. In addition, the Codex Alimentarius, an international food safety standards organization sponsored by the United Nations, adopted a guideline on assessing the safety of food from GE animals. We therefore realized it was a good time to ensure that developers, both in the U.S. and around the world, understood what FDA's regulatory requirements are regarding GE animals and food from such animals.

Q: Do GE animals look different from other animals?
A: Despite some of the doctored photographs that you may have seen circulating on the internet, adding a new gene to an animal does not result in outlandish physical combinations, such as a bird with the head of a rabbit. Genetic engineering simply doesn't work that way.

Almost all GE animals will look the same as their conventional counterparts, although there are some products in which the point of the GE process is to make the animal look slightly different (such as the GloFish).

Q: Are the offspring of a GE animal also considered GE?
A: In general, most GE animals that are being developed at this time are intended to pass their new GE traits on to their offspring. Such traits are called heritable. The initial GE animal and all of its descendants that have inherited the GE trait are called GE animals. Other GE animals have "non-heritable" traits, meaning that none of the offspring will have the trait. This guidance deals only with GE animals bearing heritable traits.

Q: *Is it possible that GE animals could displace or replace the conventional species?*
A: Over time, it is at least theoretically possible that certain GE traits might be widely adopted. For example, were ducks and chickens developed that could not carry or transmit avian influenza, it is possible that many producers of such animals, particularly in vulnerable parts of the world, would want to introduce that trait throughout their flocks. Such a trend would be no different than what already has occurred with the popular conventional livestock breeds currently used in agriculture. Such widespread adoption of any particular GE trait would likely be quite unusual.

It also would be extremely unlikely for any GE animal to accidentally displace conventional animals. Most developers of the GE animals will likely control their breeding opportunities to further their business interests. For example, GE animals producing pharmaceutical products must be carefully confined in controlled conditions, such as limited access barns, to ensure that diseases or other contaminants do not make their way into the final pharmaceutical products.

Q: *Is there a chance that this technology could be used on humans?*
A: Gene therapy has been used to attempt to treat various human diseases since 1990, and is subject to strict FDA oversight under a process different from that described in this guidance. Human gene therapy is currently limited to non-heritable therapies; that is, people who receive the new genes as part of the gene therapy can't pass them on to their children. To date there have been no gene therapies approved for humans, although several clinical trials are ongoing.

Q: *What exactly does the review process of a GE animal entail?*
A: The guidance recommends a review process that includes seven categories:

- *Product definition:* a broad statement characterizing the GE animal and the claim being made for the GE animal;

- *Molecular characterization of the construct:* a description of the rDNA construct or other genomic alteration and how they are produced;
- *Molecular characterization of the GE animal lineage:* a description of the method by which the rDNA construct or other genomic alteration was introduced into the animal and whether they are stably maintained over time;
- *Phenotypic characterization of the GE animal:* comprehensive data on the characteristics of the GE animal and its health;
- *Durability plan:* the sponsor's plan to demonstrate that the alteration will remain the same over time, and continue to have the same effect;
- *Environmental and food/feed safety:* the assessment of any environmental impacts, and for GE animals of food species, an assessment of the safety of food derived from those GE animals is safe to eat for humans and/or animals;
- *Claim validation:* a demonstration that the GE animal has the characteristics that the developer says it has.

Q: When will the first approvals be granted?

A: FDA has approved three GE animal-related applications. The first was in 2009, when FDA's Center for Veterinary Medicine approved a GE goat that produced a human biologic in its milk. The Center for Biologics Evaluation and Research approved the human biologic, ATryn. In November 2015, FDA approved an application related to AquAdvantage Salmon, a GE Atlantic salmon. In December 2015, FDA's Center for Veterinary Medicine approved a GE chicken that produces a human biologic in its eggs. The Center for Drug Evaluation and Research approved the human biologic, Kanuma (sebelipase alfa). No additional applications for GE animals will be approved until FDA determines that the rDNA construct in the animals is safe for the animals and is effective, i.e., that the GE animals do indeed possess the traits that they were intended to express, and that, if the animals are intended to be used as food, the food is safe to eat. All approvals will be handled on a case-by-case basis, and as with any approval, it is difficult to estimate how long it will take to produce the data for the agency to evaluate, and when any one of those reviews will be completed.

Q. How will FDA inform the public about new GE animals, its decisions on them, and the science behind those decisions?
A. The agency is interested in increasing the transparency of its deliberations and actions. In particular, we intend to seek input from experts and the public where there is significant public interest in an issue, and FDA believes the public may have relevant data or information to contribute. Additionally, as is the case for all NADAs, after completion of an NADA, the agency will post a Freedom of Information summary of the information in the NADA file, including information used to assess safety (to the animal and for food or feed, if appropriate) and in support of the claims made by the sponsor.

We have developed a number of consumer-appropriate publications to help inform consumers and other stakeholders about the technology and the agency's regulations of these animals. These are available on the FDA website.

FDA's new animal drug approvals (including for GE animals) are published in the Federal Register, codified in the Code of Federal Regulations, and posted on its website at Animal Drugs @ FDA. Following approvals, FDA will also provide electronic access to a summary of all information (other than confidential business or trade secret information) used in FDA's decisions as part of the freedom of information summary routinely published upon approval.

Q: What about the ethics of genetically engineering animals?
A: The issue of ethics is an extremely complicated one. On the one hand, the standard for approval does not explicitly include ethics—FDA must regulate on the basis of safety and effectiveness. However, many people would consider animal health and safety to be a subcategory of the broader term "ethics." To that end, the regulatory approach described in this guidance closely examines

animal health and requires a finding of safety to animals, and so we believe that we are addressing those particular concerns.

We do, however, recognize that genetically engineering animals may raise non-scientific social concerns that may fall under the heading of "ethics." We note that these issues are not within the scope of the guidance. We do, however, continue to participate in various venues in which these issues are discussed so that we can ensure that the discussions are based on fact and not on erroneous assumptions regarding the technology or its outcomes.

Q: Where can I get more information about genetic engineering and the GE Guidance for Industry?
A: The Guidance for Industry is available on FDA's website.

Genetically Engineering Animals Can Provide High-Quality Food

Aaron Saenz

Aaron Saenz is a former senior editor at Singularity Hub, a news website that covers the technology industry.

It's been more than a decade since humans have cracked their own genetic code, but we've yet to wake up to a world of engineered lifeforms on the Island of Dr. Moreau. While we're waiting for genetic science to mature maybe we should take a good long look at cows. Specifically, the Belgian Blue. This muscle bound meathead is a monument to the genetic power of selective breeding. A single genetic defect, a faulty myostatin gene, is responsible for its enormous bulk, and that defect was carefully passed on through the breed for more than a century before it was even known what was causing the cattle's impressive "double muscling." Watch the introduction to life of the modern Belgian Blue in [a] video from National Geographic. Before we dive into modifying the human gene pool, we better learn the lessons that working with the Belgian Blue has taught us: even the most primitive genetic tools are immensely powerful, they raise serious ethical concerns, and their results are so impressive as to almost guarantee their use. With genetic testing on the rise, and artificial insemination more prevalent, sex is primed to undergo a major renaissance in the years before it's outdone by genetic engineering.

For those who have never seen a Belgian Blue in person, the experience is...dramatic. Imagine walking past a dozen or so regular bulls and being intimidated by their sheer size and strength. Then imagine passing a bull so heavily laden with muscle it makes all those scary bulls look like cupcakes. That's the Belgian Blue, and

"Belgian Blues Will Blow Your Minds, These Cows Are Totally Ripped," Aaron Saenz, Singularity Hub, July 13, 2011. Reprinted by permission.

despite the breeds docility, it never fails to impress onlookers as a very frightening animal.

In [an audio clip] we hear about some of the amazing advantages associated with the Belgian Blue strain. They can have 40% or more additional edible muscle mass, most of which is lean meat! They gain weight well, and quickly, and produce high protein milk for their young. While they comprise a relatively small percentage of the international market, the meat itself is highly prized as its lean nature makes it healthier (and some say more tender and juicy as well).

What the breeder in the National Geographic video doesn't have time to outline is the physical problems associated with uninhibited muscle growth. The Belgian Blue and the Piedmontese, another breed with myostatin problems, are viable farm strains of cattle. They can live, reproduce, give milk, and be consumed with no risk to humans. To themselves, however, these Conan-looking cows are less friendly. They experience a wide range of health risks associated with their muscle—calves can develop enlarged tongues and stiff legs which make it difficult, if not impossible, to feed, leading to early death. Many of the cattle develop cardio-respiratory ailments. In almost all modern herds, Caesarean sections are common due to complications in pregnancy, and in some cases C-section rates have climbed to nearly 90% of all births!

Both the impressive bulk and health issues of the Belgian Blue have been maintained through the relatively simple technology of line breeding. Essentially, a very few bulls are selected to be the fathers for calves in all of the females. By choosing those bulls which clearly demonstrate the myostatin defect phenotype, breeders can make more and more of the muscled cattle. Once semen is collected from bulls (as the video so graciously shows us—eww) it can be tested and then used to impregnate cows through artificial insemination. Anecdotally it is suggested that most of the world's current Belgian Blue herds were derived from just three bulls and their descendants. While that may be an exaggeration, the truth is certainly that in efforts to perfect the breed very few male genetic lines are allowed to continue.

That's true for all types of cattle and livestock, really. Traditional selective breeding pushes us towards a narrower gene pool. It's unclear if that is going to get much worse or much better as modern genetic testing takes hold. We've already discussed how cheaper DNA tests are allowing cattle breeders to choose the absolute best bulls for line breeding. Those cheap tests mean that any rancher can now see if they have a prize bull. That may open up breeders to using new fathers, or it may simply replace the very small number of current stud bulls with a new, but equally small, generation of replacements.

Either way, what's good for cattle is slowly becoming good for humans. Though no one seems to want to phrase it in this way, humans are starting to adopt selective breeding habits and technologies. There are now several companies that sell genetic tests in association with in vitro fertilization (IVF) clinics. With good cause, I might add. Successful testing for Tay-Sachs has helped dramatically reduce the occurence of that disease in the US. Most of these newer genetic testing companies are looking to repeat that success for more than a hundred other genetic conditions. Wouldn't you want to know before you got pregnant if your children would be at high risk for crippling ailments? If you are a genetic carrier for such a disease then Preimplantation Genetic Diagnosis (PGD) can allow you to select fertilized embryos without the disease. IVF and PGD are giving us the tools necessary to, at least in terms of our own gametes, become selective breeders. Breeders informed with rudimentary genetic information, which is a step up from those Belgian farmers who first started propagating their mutant cows.

We've discussed before how genetically engineered animals are on the horizon and could be on our plates in the near future. The Belgian Blue's mutant myostatin gene variation has even been spliced into rainbow trout to give them more bulk (and thus more more worth as food). Animals are already being genetically engineered, and if work in primates is any indication, we're slowly approaching the time when scientists will be able to waltz inside a human embryo, tinker with its DNA, and get the child to come to term. That possibility, however, scares the sh*t out of most people, and angers the rest. The chances that human genetic engineering is going to have a smooth transition into becoming a popular technology is almost nil. Expect legal and social hurdles to abound. Hell, I wouldn't be surprised if armed conflict arose around this controversy as well. It could take decades before we accept such technology, though my bet is eventually that we will.

Meanwhile, modern sex powers on. PGD and IVF aren't universally excepted, but they aren't fueling riots either. Morally, they are a much more widely acceptable technology. Personally, I know a few IVF (possibly even PGD) kids and my world would be a lot poorer if they weren't around. I'm glad it's an option for parents.

But that doesn't keep it from being a stepping stone to some pretty amazing selective breeding opportunities that could give us the equivalent of designer babies even without genetic engineering. See the Belgian Blue? That's a single mutant gene that turned out to be helpful, and that simple breeding habit was propagated for more than a century. We've already seen human children who were born with the equivalent of the myostatin defect seen in the monstrous cattle. Picture a time when we discover other, relatively rare but potentially advantageous, genetic mutations. Imagine if everyone had the ability to comb through their sperm and find those mutant gametes with the desired traits you want. You could optimize your offspring—give yourself super babies with no genetic tampering required. Long before genetics is ready to replace it with something better, sexual reproduction is going to get more and more impressive thanks to modern technology.

I look forward to seeing all your Belgian Blue-like children in the future.

Genetic Engineering Can Fight Disease in Animals

Bill Pohlmeier and Alison Van Eenennaam

Bill Pohlmeier is the physiology lab manager at the University of Nebraska, Lincoln.

Alison Van Eenennaam is a cooperative extension specialist in animal genomics and biotechnology at the University of California, Davis.

Animal disease is a major social and economic problem across the United States, and throughout the world. Diseases can lead to animal suffering and distress, reduced performance, and possibly even death. Infectious diseases have major negative effects on poultry and livestock production, both in terms of economics and on animal welfare. The costs of animal disease are estimated to be 35-50% of turnover within the livestock sector in developing countries, and 17% in the developed world. Often animal disease is fought through vaccination or the use of antibiotics. However, the use of antibiotic in animal agriculture is meeting increased disapproval among consumers. In addition to enhancing animal well-being, improving animal health has the added benefit of reducing the need for veterinary interventions and the use of antibiotics and other medicinal treatments.

Animal biotechnology offers a number of approaches to fight disease in animals. Firstly, through genetic selection, livestock producers can select for certain genetic variations which have been associated with disease resistance. Through careful selection, they can develop populations of animals that are less vulnerable to disease. Secondly, through genetic engineering, breeders can integrate disease resistance genes from new sources, allowing for improved animal health. Disease resistance benefits not only

"Potential Effects of Biotechnology on Animal Health and Well-being," by Bill Pohlmeier and Alison Van Eenennaam, Applications of Animal Biotechnology in Animal Health, January 2009. Reprinted by permission.

livestock producers and their animals, but consumers also benefit as a result of safer animal products in the market place, and a reduction in the incidence of human-transmissible diseases such as avian influenza. Cattle are one species that could benefit from selection for disease resistance. Major diseases affecting cattle include foot and mouth disease, mad cow disease, mastitis, shipping fever, and brucellosis.

Disease Resistance through Genetic Selection

One method to increase disease resistance in a population of animals is to select animals which show resistance to a disease to be the parents of future generations. In this way, animals with specific genetic variations associated with disease resistance can pass those genetics on to their offspring, thus increasing the likelihood that their offspring will be resistant to infection. It has long been known that mice carrying a certain version (allele) of the Mx gene show resistance to influenza infection,[1] with the certain allele responsible for resistance known as Mx1.[2] A homologous, or similar, Mx gene has been identified in swine.[3] In vitro studies reveal that certain forms of the swine Mx gene confer different levels of resistance to influenza infection,[4] and it is thought that future in vivo studies will reveal whether selection for a certain form of swine Mx gene results in influenza resistance within a swine population. Major diseases affecting pigs include foot and mouth disease, influenza, swine fever, respiratory and wasting diseases.

Chickens are a natural host for avian influenza. As such, influenza infection in chickens can lead to sickness and even death. As with mice and swine, an Mx gene has been identified in chickens.[5, 6] In vitro studies show that certain copies of the chicken Mx gene display different levels of antiviral activity,[7] suggesting that certain populations of chickens might be less susceptible to avian influenza infection, based on their genetic background. However, similar to swine, in vivo studies will be required to determine whether live chickens actually display resistance to influenza infection based on their copy of Mx. Chicken is another species that could benefit from increased disease resistance. Major diseases affecting chickens include avian influenza, Newcastle, and Marek's diseases.

Disease-resistant Genetically Engineered Animals

While selection for disease resistance in livestock species might prove to be a powerful tool for livestock producers, it is limited by the natural genetic variation present in the species being selected. Genetic engineering, on the other hand, allows for the introduction of novel genetic sequences into the species of interest and is not limited by species barriers as the genetic building blocks in all species are the same. The use of genetic engineering has long been suggested as a method to increase disease resistance in livestock,[8] and scientists are currently working on a number of different animal models which could be used to help livestock resist infection (Table 1).

Spongiform encephalopathies, such as scrapie in sheep, and Bovine Spongiform Encephalopathy (BSE) also known as "Mad Cow Disease" in cattle are neurodegenerative diseases caused by the misfolding of a prion protein. BSE has been linked to the human neurodegenerative disease called variant Creutzfeldt Jakob disease,[27, 28] and is thus a potential threat to human health. In a procedure known as gene knockout, scientists can target a specific gene in an organism and remove it. This technology was successfully used to "knockout" the gene which codes for the prion protein in goats,[9] sheep,[10] and cattle.[11, 12] In addition to generating livestock which are free from the threat of spongiform encephalopathies, these animals could be used as a "prion-free" source of biological products for use in human medicine. Transgenic goats carrying lentivectors that express siRNAs against the prion protein have been reported.[15] RNAi is a sequence-specific method to selectively knock down endogenous gene expression. It works by introducing transgenic homologous double-stranded gene constructs which enable the stable expression of small interfering (si)RNAs that constitutively suppress target gene expression.[29]

Table 1. Extant and envisioned application for the production of disease-resistant genetically engineered livestock.

EXTANT APPLICATIONS	SPECIES	GENE	APPROACH	REFERENCE
BSE resistance	Cattle, Sheep, Goats	Prion	Knockout	9-12
Mastitis resistance	Cattle	Lysostaphin	Transgene overexpression	13
Mastitis resistance	Cattle	Lactoferrin	Transgene overexpression	14
BSE resistance	Goat	Prion	RNAi transgene	15
Visna virus resistance	Sheep	Visna virus envelope gene	Transgene overexpression	16
Mastitis resistance	Goat	Lysozyme	Transgene overexpression	17, 18
GCH virus resistance	Grass Carp	Lactoferrin	Transgene overexpression	19
Bacterial resistance	Channel Catfish	Cecropin B gene	Transgene overexpression	20
ENVISIONED APPLICATIONS	SPECIES	GENE	APPROACH	REFERENCE
Suppressing infectious pathogens	Various	RNA viruses (eg. foot and mouth, fowl plague, swine fever)	RNAi	21, 22
Coronavirus resistance	Swine	Aminopeptidase N	RNAi / Knockout	23
Avian flu resistance	Poultry	Avian influenza	RNAi	24, 25
Brucellosis resistance	Cattle	NRAMP1	Transgene overexpression	26

This approach may be a highly efficient approach to generate GE animals with targeted gene knockouts in the future, including GE animals that can knockdown infections caused by important contagious RNA viruses such as foot and mouth disease, classic swine fever, and fowl plague.[21]

Mastitis, or the infection of the mammary gland, is a disease which costs the US Dairy industry ~$2 Billion a year.[30] In an effort to reduce the effect of mastitis, scientists have developed genetically engineered cattle which are resistant to mastitis infection.[13] These cattle contain a transgene which encodes for the protein lysostaphin, which cleaves the cell wall of the bacteria which cause mastitis. Transgenic cattle produce the lysostaphin transgene in their mammary gland, which then breaks down infectious bacteria present within the gland and results in a healthier mammary gland. Similar studies using a human lysozyme transgene have demonstrated that the direction of transgene expression to the mammary gland in goats can result in reduced mastitis-causing bacteria.[17] The benefits of genetically engineered animals with disease resistance are two-fold. Firstly, they result in a healthier mammary gland, thus reducing pain and discomfort in the animals. Secondly, with reduced mammary infection, the milk, and milk products from these animals are going to be healthier, as harmful bacteria are reduced.

Research using genetic engineering to improve disease resistance is also being conducted on aquaculture species. Transgenic catfish have been developed which contain the cecropin B gene from the moth *Hyalophora cecropia*.[20] Cecropin is a small molecule that has shown anti-microbial properties, specifically against many of the bacteria that are harmful to catfish. When transgenic catfish were challenged with a form of E coli, statistically more transgenic fish survived than their non-transgenic counterparts, suggesting that expression of the transgene does indeed confer disease resistance. A disease with the potential to be treated through genetic engineering is brucellosis. Brucellosis, caused by the Brucella bacteria, is a zoonotic disease, meaning it can be ready passed between animals of different species. The animal population in and around the Yellowstone region in northwest Wyoming provides a prime example of how easily brucellosis can be spread. A number of large animal species (American Bison, Elk, etc.) in this area suffer from brucellosis.

When these infected animals come into contact with grazing cattle, the disease is readily passed. Cattle infected with brucellosis often suffer abortions, reduced fertility, and decreased milk production. In addition, brucellosis can also be passed to humans (known as undulant fever) who come into contact with infected animals, and the results can be severe. Recently a link has been established between brucellosis resistance and a variant of the bovine NRAMP1 gene.[26] Through genetic engineering, cattle could be produced which highly express the disease resistant version of NRAMP1, thus increasing their resistance to brucellosis.

A major goal of livestock and poultry breeding programs continues to be the identification of disease resistance genes, and genes that enhance immune response. There are a variety of animal biotechnologies that could be used to assist in the pursuit of this goal. Genomic selection and advanced breeding programs provide methods to identify naturally-occurring variation in disease-resistance attributes, while genetic engineering provides an approach to introduce new sources of disease resistance genes into populations. Collectively these technologies have the potential to align animal production systems with sustainability goals such as improved animal well-being due to lower disease incidence, reduced human health risk from zoonotic diseases (e.g. Mad Cow Disease, Avian Influenza, Brucellosis), and the production of safer food due to the decreased use of antibiotics and other medicinal treatments.

PEER-REVIEWED REFERENCES CITED

1. Horisberger,M.A. & Hochkeppel,H.K. An interferon-induced mouse protein involved in the mechanism of resistance to influenza viruses. Its purification to homogeneity and characterization by polyclonal antibodies. *J. Biol. Chem.* **260**, 1730-1733 (1985).

2. Staeheli,P., Grob,R., Meier,E., Sutcliffe,J.G., & Haller,O. Influenza virus-susceptible mice carry Mx genes with a large deletion or a nonsense mutation. *Mol. Cell Biol.* **8**, 4518-4523 (1988).

3. Muller,M., Winnacker,E.L., & Brem,G. Molecular cloning of porcine Mx cDNAs: new members of a family of interferon-inducible proteins with homology to GTP-binding proteins. *J. Interferon Res.* **12**, 119-129 (1992).

4. Palm,M., Leroy,M., Thomas,A., Linden,A., & Desmecht,D. Differential anti-influenza activity among allelic variants at the Sus scrofa Mx1 locus. *J. Interferon Cytokine Res.* **27**, 147-155 (2007).

5. Schumacher,B., Bernasconi,D., Schultz,U., & Staeheli,P. The chicken Mx promoter contains an ISRE motif and confers interferon inducibility to a reporter gene in chick and monkey cells. *Virology* **203**, 144-148 (1994).

6. Bernasconi,D., Schultz,U., & Staeheli,P. The interferon-induced Mx protein of chickens lacks antiviral activity. *J. Interferon Cytokine Res.* **15**, 47-53 (1995).

7. Ko,J.H. et al. Polymorphisms and the differential antiviral activity of the chicken Mx gene. *Genome Res.* **12**, 595-601 (2002).

8. Muller,M. & Brem,G. Intracellular, genetic or congenital immunisation—transgenic approaches to increase disease resistance of farm animals. *J. Biotechnol.* **44**, 233-242 (1996).

9. Yu,G.H. et al. Functional disruption of the prion protein gene in cloned goats. *Journal of General Virology* **87**, 1019-1027 (2006).

10. Denning,C. et al. Deletion of the alpha(1,3) galactosyl transferase (GGTA1) gene and the prion protein (PrP) gene in sheep. *Nature Biotechnology* **19**, 559-562 (2001).

11. Richt,J.A. et al. Production and characterization of prion protein-deficient cattle. *Transgenic Research* **16**, 842-843 (2007).

12. Richt,J.A. et al. Production of cattle lacking prion protein. *Nature Biotechnology* **25**, 132-138 (2007).

13. Wall,R.J. et al. Genetically enhanced cows resist intramammary Staphylococcus aureus infection. *Nature Biotechnology* **23**, 445-451 (2005).

14. van Berkel,P.H. et al. Large scale production of recombinant human lactoferrin in the milk of transgenic cows. *Nat Biotechnol.* **20**, 484-487 (2002).

15. Golding,M.C., Long,C.R., Carmell,M.A., Hannon,G.J., & Westhusin,M.E. Suppression of prion protein in livestock by RNA interference. *Proceedings of the National Academy of Sciences of the United States of America* **103**, 5285-5290 (2006).

16. Clements,J.E. et al. Development of transgenic sheep that express the visna virus envelope gene. *Virology* **200**, 370-380 (1994).

17. Maga,E.A., Cullor,J.S., Smith,W., Anderson,G.B., & Murray,J.D. Human lysozyme expressed in the mammary gland of transgenic dairy goats can inhibit the growth of bacteria that cause mastitis and the cold-spoilage of milk. *Foodborne Pathog. Dis.* **3**, 384-392 (2006).

18. Maga,E.A. et al. Production and processing of milk from transgenic goats expressing human lysozyme in the mammary gland. *Journal of Dairy Science* **89**, 518-524 (2006).

19. Zhong,J.Y., Wang,Y.P., & Zhu,Z.Y. Introduction of the human lactoferrin gene into grass carp (Ctenopharyngodon idellus) to increase resistance against GCH virus. *Aquaculture* **214**, 93- 101 (2002).

20. Dunham,R.A. et al. Enhanced bacterial disease resistance of transgenic channel catfish Ictalurus punctatus possessing cecropin genes. *Marine Biotechnology* **4**, 338-344 (2002).

21. Clark,J. & Whitelaw,B. A future for transgenic livestock. *Nat. Rev. Genet.* **4**, 825-833 (2003).

22. Whitelaw,C.B. & Sang,H.M. Disease-resistant genetically modified animals. *Rev Sci. Tech* **24**, 275-283 (2005).

23. Schwegmann-Wessels,C., Zimmer,G., Laude,H., Enjuanes,L., & Herrler,G. Binding of transmissible gastroenteritis coronavirus to cell surface sialoglycoproteins. *Journal of Virology* **76**, 6037-6043 (2002).

24. Sang,H. Transgenic chickens—methods and potential applications. *Trends Biotechnol.* **12**, 415- 420 (1994).

25. Tompkins,S.M., Lo,C.Y., Tumpey,T.M., & Epstein,S.L. Protection against lethal influenza virus challenge by RNA interference in vivo. *Proceedings of the National Academy of Sciences of the United States of America* **101**, 8682-8686 (2004).

26. Barthel,R. et al. Stable transfection of the bovine NRAMP1 gene into murine RAW264.7 cells: effect on Brucella abortus survival. *Infect. Immun.* **69**, 3110-3119 (2001).

27. Hill,A.F. et al. The same prion strain causes vCJD and BSE. *Nature* **389**, 448-50, 526 (1997).

28. Bruce,M.E. et al. Transmissions to mice indicate that "new variant" CJD is caused by the BSE agent. *Nature* **389**, 498-501 (1997).

29. Martin,S.E. & Caplen,N.J. Applications of RNA Interference in Mammalian Systems.* *Annual Review of Genomics and Human Genetics* **8**, 81-108 (2007).

30. Sordillo,L.M. & Streicher,K.L. Mammary gland immunity and mastitis susceptibility. *J. Mammary. Gland. Biol. Neoplasia.* **7**, 135-146 (2002).

Genetically Modifying Animals Causes Serious Health Problems

Compassion in World Farming

Compassion in World Farming is a nonprofit organization headquartered in the UK that campaigns and lobbies to improve the welfare of livestock.

Scientific research shows that cloning and genetic manipulation (GM) entail serious health and welfare problems for cloned and GM animals as well as for the surrogate mothers who carry them to birth.

Cloning and GM would take agriculture in the wrong direction, perpetuating industrial farming. This involves the use of animals selected for such high yields and growth rates that they are vulnerable to damaging health problems. Cloning and GM are out of step with the growing recognition of the need to respect animals as sentient beings.

NEW REPORT

To gain the most up-to-date knowledge on the production and use of cloned and genetically-engineered animals, Compassion in World Farming commissioned a report by animal welfare experts, Professor Don Broom and Dr Richard Kirkden from Cambridge University.[1] The report, *The Welfare of Genetically Modified and Cloned Animals Used for Food*, provides a comprehensive assessment of recent work in this field.*

The full report shows that:

* high rates of pre- and post-natal mortality and poor health are common in cloned cattle and sheep

"Cloning and Genetic Engineering of Animals for Food Production," CIWF.org. Reprinted by permission.

- the health problems experienced by these animals include breathing difficulties, heart function insufficiency, kidney problems and an increased susceptibility to infectious disease
- the production of genetically-engineered animals can also involve the suffering and death of many animals.

Cloning

Cloning aims to produce genetically identical copies of an animal.

The cloning process

The most commonly used procedure is somatic cell nuclear transfer (SCNT). This involves collecting a cell from the animal that is to be cloned (the "donor cell") and removing an egg cell from another animal. This cell is enucleated, i.e. its genetic material is removed. The donor cell and the egg cell are then fused by an electrical pulse and from this a cloned embryo is developed. This is implanted into a surrogate mother (dam).

In sheep and pigs, the transfer of the embryo into the surrogate mother is performed by a surgical procedure. In cattle, embryo transfer is sufficiently stressful that UK legislation requires a general or epidural anaesthetic.

Impact on health and welfare of surrogate dams

The European Food Safety Authority (EFSA) states that there is an increase in pregnancy failure in cattle and pigs who are carrying a clone and increased frequencies of difficult birth, especially in cattle.[2] This, together with the increased size of cloned offspring, makes Caesarean sections more frequent in cattle carrying a clone than with conventional pregnancies.

Impact on health and welfare of clones

EFSA has concluded: "The health and welfare of a significant proportion of clones … have been found to be adversely affected, often severely and with a fatal outcome."[3] Most cloned foetuses die during pregnancy or birth. Only 6-15% of cloned cattle embryos and about 6% of pig embryos are born alive . Many of these die early in life from problems such as cardiovascular failure, respiratory difficulties and defective immune systems. Of those born alive, up to 22% of cloned calves, 25% of cloned piglets and 50% of cloned lambs die before weaning.[5]

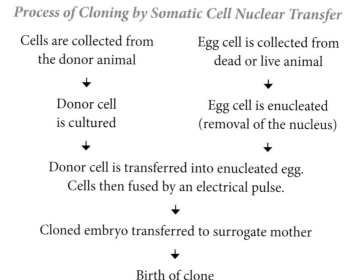

Process of Cloning by Somatic Cell Nuclear Transfer

Cells are collected from the donor animal   Egg cell is collected from dead or live animal

↓   ↓

Donor cell is cultured   Egg cell is enucleated (removal of the nucleus)

↓   ↓

Donor cell is transferred into enucleated egg. Cells then fused by an electrical pulse.

↓

Cloned embryo transferred to surrogate mother

↓

Birth of clone

European Group on Ethics

The Opinion of the European Group on Ethics (EGE) in Science and New Technologies concluded that: "Considering the current level of suffering and health problems of surrogate dams and animal clones, the EGE has doubts as to whether cloning animals for food supply is ethically justified."[6]

Use of offspring of clones on-farm

Clones will primarily be used as elite breeding animals. It is their offspring that will be farmed for meat or milk.

The likelihood is that cloning will primarily be used to produce copies of the highest yielding dairy cows and fastest growing pigs. However, traditional genetic selection has already led to major health problems for such animals. EFSA has concluded that "*genetic selection for high milk yield is the major factor causing poor welfare, in particular health problems, in dairy cows"*[7] and that genetic selection of pigs for rapid growth has led to leg disorders and cardiovascular malfunction.[8] The use of the offspring of clones on farms is likely to entrench the use of animals chosen for extreme production traits and risks perpetuating the health problems associated with such traits.

Is the incidence of pathologies and mortality declining?

Some researchers claim they are managing to reduce the incidence of ill-health and mortalities involved in cloning. A considerable body of evidence suggests that this is not the case.

In 2012 EFSA stated that no new information has become available that would lead it to reconsider the conclusions in its 2008 Opinion on the animal health and welfare aspects of cloning.[9] Unacceptable death rates of the animals involved have forced AgResearch, a leading New Zealand research organisation, to end its SCNT cloning trials.[10] A Japanese survey revealed that survival rates of transferred cloned bovine embryos and cloned calves had not improved—indeed had deteriorated—over a decade (1998–2007).[11]

Genetic Engineering

Farm animals are being genetically engineered for various purposes including enhanced growth rates, increased disease resistance and altered meat and milk composition.

Genetic engineering involves the insertion into an animal of genes from another species or extra genes from the same species. Alternatively it can entail the manipulation or knocking-out of an animal's own genes.

Enhanced growth rates

Animals that have been genetically engineered for faster growth have suffered from harmful side-effects. The production of fast-growing GM animals is most advanced in the case of farmed fish. This has led to deformities, feeding and breathing difficulties, reduced swimming abilities and lower tolerance to disease.[12]

Increased disease resistance

Conferring improved disease resistance on animals appears to be benign. However, the UN Food and Agriculture Organization points out that industrial livestock production plays an important part in the emergence and spread of diseases.[13] The proper way to address such diseases is to keep animals in less intensive systems. Good hygiene, husbandry and housing rather than genetic engineering should be used to prevent the diseases that stem from factory farming.

Altered meat and milk composition

Researchers point to the health benefits of tackling rising levels of obesity and cardiovascular disease in humans by genetically engineering animals to produce lower levels of saturated fats and higher levels of beneficial omega-3 fatty acids. However, the incidence of these problems can be reduced by improving our diet. A major study concluded that a 30% decrease in intake of saturated fats from animal sources in the UK could reduce heart disease by 15%.[14] Reduced levels of saturated fat and improved levels of omega-3 fatty acids can be achieved by replacing factory farmed chicken and grain-fed beef with free-range chicken (especially slower growing breeds) and pasture-fed beef.[15]

Policy Recommendations

In light of the adverse impact of cloning and GM on animal health and welfare, cloning and GM animals should not play any part in European farming.

The EU Should Prohibit:

- the cloning or genetic engineering of animals for food production
- the use of clones, GM animals and their offspring in the EU; this will make it pointless to import semen and embryos of clones and GM animals
- the sale of food from clones and GM animals

- the sale of food from the offspring of clones and GM animals. At the very least, such food should be labelled.

* This work was made possible by a grant from the World Society for the Protection of Animals (WSPA) and the full report is available to download from ciwf.org/cloningreport.

REFERENCES

1. Broom, D. and Kirkden, R., 2012. Welfare of Genetically Modified and Cloned Animals Used for Food.
2. EFSA, 2008. Scientific Opinion of the Scientific Committee on a request from the European Commission on Food Safety, Animal Health and Welfare and Environmental Impact of Animals derived from Cloning by Somatic Cell Nucleus Transfer (SCNT) and their Offspring and Products Obtained from those Animals. *EFSA Journal*, 767: 1-49.
3. *Ibid*
4. EFSA, 2012. Update on the state of play of Animal Health and Welfare and Environmental Impact of Animals derived from SCNT Cloning and their Offspring, and Food Safety of Products Obtained from those Animals. *EFSA Journal*, 10(7):2794.
5. Broom, D. and Kirkden, R., 2012. Welfare of Genetically Modified and Cloned Animals Used for Food.
6. European Group on Ethics in Science and New Technologies, 2008. Ethical aspects of animal cloning for food supply. Opinion No. 23.
7. EFSA, 2009. Scientific Opinion on the overall effects of farming systems on dairy cow welfare and disease. *EFSA Journal*, 1143, 1-38.
8. EFSA, 2007. Animal health and welfare in fattening pigs in relation to housing and husbandry. *EFSA Journal*, 564, 1-14.
9. As 4
10. Reported in New Zealand press and confirmed as accurate by New Zealand Ministry of Agriculture.
11. Watanabe S. and Nagai T., 2011. Survival of embryos and calves derived from somatic cell nuclear transfer in cattle: a nationwide survey in Japan. *Animal Science Journal*, 82, 360-365.
12. Compassion in World Farming and WSPA, 2007. Closed Waters: The welfare of farmed atlantic salmon, rainbow trout, atlantic cod & atlantic halibut.
13. Otte, J. *et al*, 2007. Industrial Livestock Production and Global Health Risks. Pro-Poor Livestock Policy Initiative.
14. Friel *et al*, 2009. Public health benefits of strategies to reduce greenhouse-gas emissions: food and agriculture. *The Lancet*, 374 (9706), 2016 – 2025.
15. Compassion in World Farming, 2012. Nutritional benefits of higher welfare animal products. ciwf.org/nutrition.

Many Issues with GM Animals Still Debated

Yourgenome.org

Yourgenome.org is a source of information about genetics sponsored by the Public Engagement team at the Wellcome Genome Campus in the UK.

Genetic engineering refers to the direct manipulation of an organism's genes to alter or enhance certain characteristics.

The number of genetically modified animals used in agriculture has increased significantly in recent years. Researchers have genetically engineered a number of mammals, from laboratory animals to farm animals, as well as birds, fish and insects.

The most widely used genetically modified animals are laboratory animals, such as the fruitfly (*Drosophila*) and mice. Genetically engineered animals enable scientists to gain an insight into basic biological processes and the relationships between mutations and disease.

However, farm animals, such as sheep, goats and cows, can also be genetically modified to enhance specific characteristics. These can include milk production and disease resistance, as well as improving the nutritional value of the products they are farmed for. For example, cows, goats and sheep have been genetically engineered to express specific proteins in their milk.

The majority of work on genetically modified farm animals is still in the research phase and is yet to be used commercially. Below are some of the advantages and disadvantages associated with genetically modifying animals for agriculture, divided up into four key areas:

"Is it ethical to genetically modify farm animals for agriculture?" Debate, yourgenome.org, Reprinted by permission.

- Do the benefits of genetically modified farm animals outweigh the risks?
- Is genetic modification of farm animals ethical?
- Is it morally acceptable to genetically modify farm animals?
- Is there a thorough regulatory process for genetic modification of farm animals?

Do the benefits of genetically modified farm animals outweigh the risks?

Yes

- Genetic engineering holds great potential in many fields, including agriculture, medicine and industry.
- Genetic modification can increase the yield from farm animals, for example cows can be engineered to produce more milk for the same size of herd.
- Genetically modified farm animals are being used to produce important medicinal products, such as antibodies, in large quantities. These products can be used for the treatment of many different human conditions. The current production system for such products is donated human blood, which is in limited supply due to a lack of donors.
- Sheep and goats can be modified to produce medicinal products in their milk. This has no negative impact on the animal but the product can help to treat human diseases.

No

- The transfer of genetic material from one species to another raises potentially serious health issues for animals and humans.
- There is a risk that new diseases from genetically engineered animals could be spread to non-genetically engineered animals, and even humans.
- In many cases, selective breeding is just as effective as genetic engineering and doesn't carry the same risks.

- We don't yet know if eating the products of genetically modified animals could potentially harm us.

Is genetic modification of farm animals ethical?

Yes

- Genetic engineering is a logical continuation of selective breeding, which has been done by humans for thousands of years.
- Genetic engineering of animals is strictly controlled by animal cruelty legislations in many countries and is always carefully scrutinised by teams of experts before being approved for wider use.

No

- Many of the embryos that undergo genetic engineering procedures do not survive.
- Genetic modification can put animals at risk of harm. For example, transgenic pigs were found to be arthritic, partially blind and infertile when a human growth hormone was inserted into their genomes to make them grow faster.

Is it morally acceptable to genetically modify farm animals?

Yes

- Not all genetic engineering directly benefits humans. Some genetic engineering is to improve resistance of livestock to disease, for example, bovine spongiform encephalopathy ("mad cow disease") in cattle. It can also be used to remove characteristics that cause injury, for example, selecting for cattle without horns.
- Animals have been used to help humans for millennia. Many would say that human lives are of higher moral value than animal lives.

- The percentage of genetically modified farm animals is tiny compared to the number of animals slaughtered for humans to eat. This practice is widely seen as morally acceptable.

No

- Research could use other organisms such as plants and bacteria to mass produce therapies for human medicine. For example, genetically engineered cereal grains to produce human proteins.
- The cost to the animal always outweighs the benefits as, by carrying out genetic engineering, we are violating their rights
- Genetic engineering often involves modifying animals for reasons that have no benefit for that species, and could potentially cause them pain and discomfort.
- We shouldn't be attempting to "play God." Life should not be regarded as a product that can be altered and played with for economic benefit.

Is there a thorough regulatory process for genetic modification of farm animals?

Yes

- It has been suggested that, as a rule, genetically engineered animals should be no worse off than the equivalent stock would be if they were not genetically engineered.
- The Animal Welfare Act, a federal law passed in the UK in 1966, requires all entities looking to carry out research with animals to have their programme reviewed before they go ahead, have veterinary care programmes in place and staff that are qualified to care for live animals.
- The UK Home Office Animals (Scientific Procedures) Act 1986 has set out guidelines for research involving animals.
- The FDA (Food and Drug Administration) in the USA regulates genetic engineering with animals and their products under the new animal drug provisions of the Federal Food,

Drug and Cosmetic Act (FFDCA). It helps monitor and maintain certain standards, including input from the public, when it comes to genetically engineering animals.

- The "new animal drug" provisions of the FFDCA focuses on whether the new animal drug is safe for the animal and if it is effective. If the drug is for a food-producing animal it also focuses on whether the resulting food is safe to eat.

No

- Genetic engineering of animals is a relatively new practice and is mainly used in research. As a result regulations for its use in farming are minimal.
- For regulations that have been put in place for the use of animals in research, it is often unclear how they would be applied to genetic engineering of farm animals and few guidelines refer to it directly.

Organizations to Contact

The editors have compiled the following list of organizations concerned with the issues debated in this book. The descriptions are derived from materials provided by the organizations. All have publications or information available for interested readers. This list was compiled on the date of publication of the present volume; the information provided here may change. Be aware that many organizations take several weeks or longer to respond to inquiries, so allow as much time as possible.

American Society for Human Genetics (ASHG)
9650 Rockville Pike
Bethesda, MD 20814-3998
(301) 634-7300
email: society@ashg.org
website: http://www.ashg.org

The American Society of Human Genetics (ASHG) is the primary professional membership organization for human genetics specialists worldwide. ASHG provides forums for advancing genetic research, improving genetics education, and promoting responsible scientific policies. ASHG publishes the *American Journal of Human Genetics* and the electronic newsletter *SNP-IT*.

American Society of Law, Medicine & Ethics (ASLME)
765 Commonwealth Avenue, Suite 1634
Boston, MA 02215
(617) 262-4990
email: infor@aslme.org
website: http://www.aslme.org

The American Society of Law, Medicine & Ethics (ASLME) is a nonprofit educational organization focused on the intersection of law, medicine, and ethics. ASLME provides a forum for the exchange of ideas to protect public health, reduce health disparities, promote quality of care, and facilitate dialogue on emerging science. ASLME publishes the *Journal of Law, Medicine & Ethics* and *American Journal of Law & Medicine.*

Biotechnology Innovation Organization (BIO)
1201 Maryland Avenue SW, Suite 900
Washington, DC 20024
(202) 962-9200
email: info@bio.org
website: http://www.bio.org

The Biotechnology Innovation Organization (BIO) is a trade association representing biotechnology companies, academic institutions, state biotechnology centers, and related organizations worldwide. Its members are involved in the research and development of innovative health care, agricultural, industrial, and environmental biotechnology products. BIO publishes *BIOtechNOW* and the *BIO Newsletter.*

Center for Food Safety (CFS)
660 Pennsylvania Avenue SE, Suite 301
Washington, DC 20003
(202) 547-9359
email: office@centerforfoodsafety.org
website: http://www.centerforfoodsafety.org

Center for Food Safety (CFS) is a nonprofit public interest and environmental advocacy organization It works to protect human health and the environment by curbing the use of harmful food production technologies and by promoting organic and other forms of sustainable agriculture. CFS also educates consumers concerning the definition of organic food and products. CFS uses legal actions, groundbreaking scientific and policy reports, books and other educational materials, market pressure, and grass roots campaigns. CFS educates consumers concerning the definition of organic food and products. Available on its website are fact sheets, newsletters, reports, and policy statements on food and agricultural issues.

Center for Genetics and Society (CGS)

1122 University Avenue, Suite 100
Berkeley, CA 94702
(510) 665-7760
email: info@geneticsandsociety.org
website: http://www.geneticsandsociety.org

The Center for Genetics and Society is a nonprofit information and public affairs organization working to encourage responsible uses and effective oversight of human genetic and reproductive technologies and other emerging technologies. CGS works with a network of scientists, health professionals, and civil society leaders to oppose applications of new human genetic and reproductive technology applications that objectify and commodify human life and threaten to divide human society. CGS publishes *Biopolitical Times* and *Biopolitical Views & News*, available on its website.

Council for Responsible Genetics (CRG)

5 Upland Road, Suite 3
Cambridge, MA 02140
(617) 868-0870
email: crg@gene-watch.org
website: http://www.councilforresponsiblegenetics.org

The Council for Responsible Genetics is a nonprofit, non-governmental organization that fosters public debate about the social, ethical, and environmental implications of genetic technologies. CRG works through the media and concerned citizens to distribute accurate information on emerging issues in biotechnology. CRG also publishes a bimonthly magazine, *GeneWatch*, which monitors biotechnology's social, ethical, and environmental consequences.

Ethics and Public Policy Center (EPPC)
1730 M Street NW, Suite 910
Washington, DC 20036
(202) 682-1200
email: ethics@eppc.org
website: http://www.eppc.org

The Ethics and Public Policy Center (EPPC) is dedicated to applying the Judeo-Christian moral tradition to critical issues of public policy. EPPC defends and promotes our nation's founding principles—respect for the inherent dignity of the human person, individual freedom and responsibility, justice, the rule of law, and limited government. Its website provides a searchable database of commentaries by its scholars.

Food & Water Watch
1616 P Street NW, Suite 300
Washington, DC 20036
(202) 683-2500
email: info@fwwatch.org
website: http://www.foodandwaterwatch.org

Food & Water Watch is a public interest organization that promotes policies that lead to healthy food, safe and affordable drinking water, and sustainable energy. Its website provides a searchable policy and research library of reports, fact sheets, and case studies on such topic as GMOs and food safety.

Genetics Society of America (GSA)
9650 Rockville Pike
Bethesda, MD 20814-3998
(301) 634-7300
email: society@genetics-gsa.org
website: http://www.genetics-gsa.org

The mission of the Genetics Society of America (GSA) is to deepen the public's understanding of the living world by advancing the field of genetics. It fosters an international community of geneticists, educates students and the public, communicates new discoveries, and advocates for the continued support of genetics research. The GSA publishes two journals: *GENETICS*, and *G3: Genes|Genomes|Genetics.*

Institute for Responsible Technology
PO Box 469
Fairfield, IA 52556
(641) 209-1765
email: info@responsibletechnology.org
website: http://www.responsibletechnology.org

The Institute for Responsible Technology works to educate policy makers and the public about the dangers of genetically modified organisms (GMOs). The organization investigates and reports the impact of genetically modified food on health, environment, the economy, and agriculture, as well as the problems associated with current research, regulating, corporate practices, and reporting. The website provides reports, fact sheets, and multimedia presentations on the topic of GMOs.

International Centre for Genetic Engineering
Science Park
Padriciano 99
34149 Trieste, Italy
email: icgeb@icgeb.org
website: http://www.icgeb.org/home.html

This organization provides information regarding research in molecular biology and biotechnology that can meet the needs of the developing world. It focuses on biomedicine, crop improvement, environmental protection, and biopesticide production. Its website provides the results of its research and articles published in major scientific journals.

National Academies of Sciences, Engineering, and Medicine
500 Fifth Street NW
Washington, DC 20001
(202) 334-2000
email: worldwidewebfeedback@nas.edu
website: http://www.nationalacademies.org

These academies were established by the US government to provide scientific information and resources to members of Congress and the public. Among its areas of interest are agriculture, health and medicine, engineering and physical sciences, and policy and global affairs. Its website provides a searchable database of current and past research projects.

National Human Genome Research Institute (NHGRI)
National Institutes of Health
Building 31, Room 4B09
31 Center Drive, MSC 2152
9000 Rockville Pike
Bethesda, MD 20892-2152
(301) 402-0911
website: https://www.genome.gov

The National Human Genome Research Institute (NHGRI) was developed in collaboration with the United States Department of Energy to map the human genome. It established the Division of Intramural Research to apply genome technologies to the study of specific diseases and the genetic components of complex disorders. Its website contains many tools to facilitate the pace of biomedical research, including resources for educators, scientists, and journalists.

Union of Concerned Scientists
Two Brattle Square
Cambridge, MA 02138-3780
(617) 547-5552
website: http://www.ucsusa.org

The Union of Concerned Scientists works to build a safe and healthy world by encouraging scientific, evidence-based decision making at local, state, national, and international levels. It has played key roles in developing renewable energy sources and protection for rainforests. Its website contains blogs, publications, and reports on major environmental projects worldwide.

US Food and Drug Administration (FDA)
10903 New Hampshire Avenue
Silver Spring, MD 20993
(888) 463-6332
website: http://www.fda.gov

The Food and Drug Administration (FDA) is an agency within the US Department of Health and Human Services. The FDA is responsible for protecting public health by assuring food and drug safety. Its website provides resources and libraries on food safety, nutrition, food-relation regulations, and drug safety and research.

Bibliography

Books

Emily Anthes — *Frankenstein's Cat: Cuddling Up to Biotech's Brave New Beasts.* New York, NY: Scientific American/Farrar, Straus and Giroux, 2013.

Michael Burgan — *Genetic Engineering: Science, Technology, and Engineering* (Calling All Innovators). New York, NY: Scholastic, 2016.

Nessa Carey — *The Epigenetics Revolution.* New York, NY: Columbia University Press, 2012.

George Church and Edward Regis — *Regenesis: How Synthetic Biology Will Reinvent Nature and Ourselves.* New York, NY: Basic Books, 2012.

Marina Cohen — *Genetic Engineering* (Let's Relate to Genetics). New York, NY: Crabtree Publishing, 2010.

Steven Druker and Jane Goodall — *Altered Genes, Twisted Truth: How the Venture to Genetically Engineer Our Food Has Subverted Science, Corrupted Government, and Systematically Deceived the Public.* Salt Lake City, UT: Clear River Press, 2015.

Lillian Forman — *Genetically Modified Foods* (Essential Viewpoints). Edina, MN: ABDO Publishing, 2010.

Eve Hartman and Wendy Meshbesher — *What Are the Issues with Genetic Technology?* Chicago, IL: Raintree, 2012.

John T. Lang — *What's So Controversial About Genetically Modified Food?* London, UK: Reaktion Books, 2016.

Steven Lipkin and Jon Luoma — *The Age of Genomes: Tales from the Front Line.* Boston, MA: Beacon Press, 2016.

Salah E. Mahgoub — *Genetically Modified Foods: Basics, Applications, and Controversy,* London, UK: CRC Press, 2016.

Siddhartha Mukherjee   *The Gene: An Intimate History*. New York, NY:
                        Scribner, 2016.

Kathy Wilson Peacock   *Biotechnology and Genetic Engineering* (Global
                        Issues). New York, NY: Facts on File, 2010.

Steven Potter   *Designer Genes: A New Era in the Evolution of
                        Man*. New York, NY: Random House, 2010.

Claire Robinson and   *GMO Myths and Truths*. London, UK: Earth
Michael Antoniou   Open Source, 2015.

Tara Rodden Robinson   *Genetics for Dummies*. Hoboken, NJ: Wiley
                        Publishing, Inc., 2010.

Josh Schonwald   *The Taste of Tomorrow: Dispatches from the
                        Future of Food*. New York, NY: Harper,
                        2012.

Marcus Wohlsen   *Biopunk: Kitchen-counter Scientists Hack the
                        Software of Life*. New York, NY: Current,
                        2011.

Periodicals and Internet Sources

Jacqueline Adams   "Can Science Save Your Orange Juice?" *Science
                        World*, Vol. 71, Issue 11, April 13, 2015,
                        pp. 14–17.

Judith Benz-   "Super-muscly Pigs Trading Ethics for
Schwarzburg and   Efficiency," *Issues in Science & Technology*,
Arianna Ferrari   Vol. 32, Issue 3, Spring 2016, pp. 29–32.

Rachel Ehrenberg   "GMOs Under Scrutiny," *Science News*, Vol. 189,
                        Issue 3, February 6, 2016, pp. 22–27.

Ferris Jabr   "Building Tastier Fruits & Veggies," *Scientific
                        American*, Vol. 311, Issue 1, July 2014, pp.
                        56–61.

Melinda Wenner   "Infant Possibilities," *Popular Science*, Vol. 285,
Moyer   Issue 2, August 2014, pp. 50–85.

Russell Powell   "The Evolutionary Biological Implications of
                          Human Genetic Engineering," *Journal of
                          Medicine & Philosophy*, Vol. 37, Issue 3, June
                          2012, pp. 204–225.

William Powell   "The American Chestnut's Genetic Rebirth,"
                          Scientific American, Vol. 310, Issue 3, March
                          2014, pp. 68–73.

Antonio Regalado   "Engineering the Perfect Baby," *MIT Technology
                          Review*, May/June 2015.

Tina Hesman Saey   "Gene Drives Unleashed," *Science News*, Vol.
                          188, Issue 12, December 12, 2015, pp.
                          16–22.

Index

A

adult stem cells, 50, 52, 57, 60, 61–62
Agricultural Resource Management Survey (ARMS) (USDA), 100
American Academy of Environmental Medicine (AAEM), 106
American Association for the Advancement of Science (AAAS), 22
American Nurses Association, 106
American Public Health Association, 106
Andrew, Araromi Adewale, 28–32
Animal Welfare Act, 149

B

Bacillus thuringiensis (Bt), 83, 98–105
Belgian Blue cattle, 128–131
Bereano, Phil, 21
Berry, Wendell, 112
biological weapons, genetic engineering and, 31
biopharm animals, explanation of, 116
Blackford, Russell, 72–76
Blackwelder, Brent, 23
bovine growth hormone/bovine somatotropin (BST), 31, 106
bovine spongiform encephalopathy (BSE), 117, 133, 134, 137, 148
Broom, Don, 140
brucellosis, 133, 136–137
"bubble boy" disease, 28
Burrows, Beth, 24, 26

C

Cartagena Protocol on Biosafety, 88
cellular/molecular cloning, 60
Chapela, Ignacio, 24, 25, 26, 27
Clinton, Bill, 66
clone/cloning, definition of, 47–48
cloning of animals, 16, 46, 64, 117–118, 140, 141–143. *See also* Dolly the sheep; genetic engineering of animals
Codex Alimentarius, 84, 87–88, 90, 92, 123
companion animals, explanation of, 117
Compassion in World Farming, 140–145
conservation tillage, 103
CRISPR-CAS9, 33, 34, 35, 36, 96
cystic fibrosis, 28, 38

D

Darnovsky, Marcy, 26
Deneen, Sally, 19–27
designer babies. *See* genetic engineering of babies/designer babies
diabetes, 28
disease-resistant animals, explanation of, 117
DNA, 14, 16, 20, 23, 25, 30, 33, 34, 35, 36, 37, 48, 57, 63, 72, 73, 77, 82, 87, 106, 116, 117, 118, 119, 120, 125, 130, 131
Dolly the sheep, 16, 22, 46, 50, 63, 64, 66, 72, 73, 77

medical benefits of, 77–80
overview/definitions of, 16,
 46–53
and permanent changes to gene
 pool, 67
reasons for supporting/benefits
 of, 72–76, 78–80
see also genetic engineering
 of babies/designer babies;
 reproductive cloning;
 therapeutic cloning
Human Cloning Foundation, 80
Human Genome Organization, 47
Human Genome Project, 20, 22, 24
*Humanity Enhanced: Genetic Choice
 and the Challenge for Liberal
 Democracies*, 73, 74
Hwang Woo Suk, 51, 78

I

infertility, 16, 31, 69, 79
Institute for Responsible
 Technology, 15
International Assessment of
 Agricultural Knowledge, Science
 and Technology for Development
 (IAASTD), 109

J

Janssens, A Cecile JW, 33–36
Joy, Bill, 26

K

Kirkden, Richard, 140
Kolehmainen, Sophia M., 63–71
Kuppuswamy, Chamundeeswari,
 46–53

L

labeling of GM ingredients/food, 14,
 86, 120
Livingston, Michael, 98–105

M

Macer, Darryl, 46–53
mad cow disease. *See* bovine
 spongiform encephalopathy (BSE)
mastitis, 31, 117, 121, 133, 136
Mayes, Christopher, 111–114
Monsanto, 107, 108
Moore, G.E., 113
More, Max, 26
Musil, Robert, 23

N

Nakhooda, Muhammad, 93–97
National Academy of Sciences, 31
National Bioethics Advisory
 Commission (NBAC), 66, 70
National Research Council, 102
Newman, Stuart, 23

O

outcrossing, explanation of, 85

P

Pakhare, Jayashree, 77–80
parthenogenesis, 78
Patra, Satyajit, 28–32
Pohlmeier, Bill, 132–139